BRITAIN IN OLD PHOTOGRAPHS
AROUND
HOYLAND

including Hoyland Nether, Wentworth, Tankersley,
Stainborough, Blacker Hill & Surrounding Districts

GEOFFREY HOWSE

SUTTON PUBLISHING LIMITED

Sutton Publishing Limited
Phoenix Mill · Thrupp · Stroud
Gloucestershire · GL5 2BU

First published 1999

Reprinted 2000

Copyright © Geoffrey Howse, 1999

British Library Cataloguing in Publication Data
A catalogue record for this book is available from the British Library.

ISBN 0-7509-2268-0

Typeset in 10.5/13.5 Photina.
Typesetting and origination by
Sutton Publishing Limited.
Printed in Great Britain by
Ebenezer Baylis, Worcester.

Title page photograph: Hoyland Cinema House was built in 1920 on a site previously occupied by Hoyland Market, by a group of local businessmen who formed the Hoyland Cinema Company, which gave Hoyland its much needed third screen – such was the popularity of 'going to the pictures' during this period. The new cinema was sandwiched between the reduced market site and the Strafford Arms. It had stalls and balcony and seats upholstered in Prussian blue plush. This photograph was taken in the 1920s when the silent feature films *The Man on the Box*, starring Sydney Chaplin, and *Salome of the Tenements* were the attractions. It was the last cinema to open and the first to close: it screened its last film in 1957. The building stood empty until it was demolished in November 1971; the site is once again occupied by Hoyland Market. The iron posts in the foreground were positioned there to mark the boundary of the market when the original market opened in 1867. (*Walker's Newsagents collection*)

Looking along Market Street, Hoyland, to High Street and George Street, beside the Town Hall. On the left beyond Kelly's café can be seen the gable end of Rowland Cross's shop, and on the corner of King Street and George Street, the Globe Tea Company's premises; beyond this is the police station, built in 1889 and demolished in 1972. The buildings on the right are substantially the same in appearance today. (*Joan Masheder collection*)

CONTENTS

The Newcomen-type engine, situated in the area of Elsecar known as Distillery Side, was constructed in 1795 on an adjacent site to Earl Fitzwilliam's Elsecar New Colliery, which was sunk in the same year. This celebrated beam engine is the only engine of its type in the world which remains on its original site. Considered Elsecar's major asset, it is without doubt the most important surviving artefact of South Yorkshire's early industrial expansion. In 1927 Henry Ford paid a secret visit to Elsecar, during a tour which took in several industrial areas throughout this country. His intention was to take exhibits back to the Ford Museum in Detroit. He expressed a strong interest in the engine at Elsecar. However, someone politely pointed out to Mr Ford that the Elsecar engine was not for sale at any price. *(Chris Thawley collection)*

A view of Hoyland town centre, *c.* 1900. Bellamy's Boot Stores and Colville's grocers and tobacconists occupy the building which in 1999 is occupied by the NatWest Bank. The Wesleyan chapel, the tall fortress-like building, is on the left. This photograph looks in the opposite direction to the photograph on page 2. (*Chris Thawley collection*)

Hoyland Town Silver Prize Band won many trophies. One such trophy, shown here, was the Daily Mail Challenge Cup, won at the Belle Vue Spring Festival for Brass Bands. Taken in the 1970s, the photograph shows George Hopson, landlord of the Strafford Arms, pouring rum into the cup. Holding the cup is M. Thompson (conductor) and C. Pearson (bandmaster). (*Joan Hopson collection*)

INTRODUCTION

Within the West Riding of Yorkshire is a unique region, situated in the heart of the area known historically as South Yorkshire. Its uniqueness lies in its development over a thousand years. It is a microcosm of agricultural, architectural and industrial development, whose historical significance is without equal. The area has all the necessary elements for studying the various component parts of this model of rural and urban, agricultural and industrial development, on a scale and with a quality which can be found nowhere else in England. *Around Hoyland* sets out to show both important historic buildings and sites as they appeared over a hundred years ago and the simpler buildings where local people carried out their daily activities, where they worked, lived and played. It shows the same places in more recent times, as well as the sometimes dramatic changes which have taken place. Families who have influenced the development of the area are mentioned, and some of the local residents who have played their part in some way in shaping the area over the last hundred and fifty years are also featured.

St Peter's Church, built in 1830, viewed from Hoyland Law Stand, *c.* 1920. (*Walker's Newsagents collection*)

In the research to provide the accompanying information for the illustrations I have been fortunate in being able to draw on some excellent source material. In addition to spending time at Sheffield Archive, Barnsley Library and Westminster Reference Library, I have gathered and cross referenced information from old documents, pamphlets, diaries, letters and essays, as well as conducting personal interviews with local people. The unpublished work *Hoyland Nether*, by local historian Arthur K. Clayton BEM, has pointed me in the right direction on more than one occasion. Mr Clayton's extensive efforts over many years to produce a history of Hoyland Nether, with accompanying facts and figures, has proved invaluable in clarifying certain information. Sheila Margaret Ottley, in her book *While Martha Told the Hours*, covers many of the subjects included in the photographs of Hoyland, which has helped to identify some of the images; and Michael F. Bedford's book *Hoyland Nether through the Years* has also proved a useful reference for filling in gaps regarding names and dates.

The choice of material included has been purely personal. Wherever people appear in photographs I have attempted to identify them. With some subjects there is conflicting evidence regarding dates. I have tried to sift through evidence available to me in an attempt to provide as accurate a description as possible, and some information has been passed on by word-of-mouth, which is often interesting but in some instances may be regarded as purely anecdotal. As with identifying people, the exact identification or meaning of some subjects has not been completely possible in every case. I apologise for any errors or omissions.

One of the most encouraging aspects I have found during the compilation of this book has been the enthusiasm of many local people, many of whom have approached me with offers of photographs, information and documents. In fact, I have so much information and material available to me that I have sufficient to produce another similar book to this. Such is the variety of subjects and the diversity of the surrounding landscape, that the inclusion of every aspect of life in the area has not been possible. I hope I have managed to capture the essential essence.

I hope that *Around Hoyland*, published during this last year of the twentieth century, will help to give local people a greater appreciation of the rich and varied history of the area in which they live; and give encouragement in the new millennium to fight to preserve that which is worthy or historically important, ensuring that the destruction which has taken place in the recent past is never allowed to happen again, as well as offering a broader view of this historically and culturally interesting area to a wider public. In the pages that follow, as well as including historical fact, I make criticisms, draw comparisons and make suggestions about what might have been a better course to follow. These stem from purely personal observations and experiences, and I accept that in some instances the reader may disagree with my assertions.

CHAPTER ONE

HOYLAND NETHER

Today Hoyland Nether, which covers an area totalling 1,999 acres, consists of the township of Hoyland, Hoyland Common, Platts Common and Milton, the hamlets of Upper Hoyland and Skiers Hall and the village of Elsecar, which incorporates the areas known as St Helens, Cobar and Stubbin. Before 1938, when the revision of boundaries took place, Hoyland Nether covered 2,082 acres 3 roods and 39.7 perches. Until then, part of Harley, Alderthwaite and Skiers fell within the Hoyland boundary and are mentioned as early as the 13th century. In 1938 the Harley portion was given to Rotherham Rural District. In exchange, land in Brampton Bierlow, which included the site of Elsecar Main Colliery, became part of Hoyland Nether.

The name Hoyland is believed to have its origins in either the Danish word 'hoi', which means hill-land, or the old Norse word 'haugr' meaning a hill. This is not surprising, as place names throughout Yorkshire were influenced by the Viking invaders. During the reign of Edward the Confessor (1042–66) Hoyland was owned by three Saxon earls, Harold, Reder and Swen. After the Norman Conquest in 1066 William I transferred many of the Saxon estates to Norman ownership. Although Swen continued to own some land in the area, Hoyland was partly owned by Roger de Busli from Tickhill Castle and William De Warene of Conisborough Castle. The name Nether was added a long time afterwards, as there were two places with the name of Hoyland less than 10 miles apart, and this obviously led to confusion. The two became Hoyland Nether and High Hoyland. From the time of the Domesday Survey, when it is mentioned as Hoiland, until the beginning of the 18th century, like many places in the West Riding Hoyland consisted of a series of scattered farms, smallholdings and cottages. It was in the parish of Wath-upon-Dearne and had no place of worship within its boundaries. In the 1720s the Townend family, prominent yeoman farmers from Upper Hoyland, had Hoyland Chapel constructed, and it was consecrated in 1740. St Peter's Church replaced this chapel in 1830, and acted as a chapel of ease until it acquired its own parish in 1855. Various chapels opened throughout the district during the years that followed. Hoyland's population continued to increase and by 1890 a second church, St Andrew's, had opened for worship. Originally a chapel of ease to St Peter's, it was given its own parish in 1916.

During the reign of Richard II in 1379, fifty-eight people over the age of sixteen were subjected to the Poll Tax in Hoyland, levied to raise money following the wars with Scotland and France. The settlement gradually evolved into a small town, and by 1830 had its own post office. By 1838 a postal service was running three days a week between the Gate Inn and Barnsley, which was at that time on the mail coach route between Leeds and London. Hoyland Nether grew and prospered. This was to no small extent because of the benevolence of the noble family residing at Wentworth Woodhouse, on whose land most of the township had grown, or through whose enterprise and influence much investment was made throughout the area. In 1801 Hoyland had a population of 823 people. By 1851 the population had increased to 2,912 and by 1901 to 12,464.

Hoyland market opened on 28 May 1858 and there were parades and feasting to mark the occasion. In 1891 a Local Board was formed to run the affairs of the growing community. Its headquarters were in the Town Hall, a building which had been constructed in 1840 to serve as a Mechanics' Institute. A well-known local resident and businesswoman, Martha Knowles, donated to the township a clock and a tower to house it, and this was added to the Town Hall. Only three years after its formation the board was replaced by an Urban District Council, under the terms of the 1894 Local Government Act. This council survived until the major local government changes of 1974, when Hoyland Nether UDC was absorbed into the Metropolitan Borough of Barnsley.

The transformation of Hoyland into what it has become at the end of the 20th century has largely occurred in the last thirty years. The destruction of three-quarters of the town centre has, without doubt, completely ruined the appearance of this once attractive, albeit grimy, Yorkshire town. It occurred when the trend to tear down old buildings and replace them with utilitarian modern structures was at its height. Little or no consideration was given to the prospect of restoring Georgian and early Victorian buildings, or to changing their use. Mining subsidence was an all too regularly used excuse for pulling buildings down. People accepted it. If a building was damaged, it was cheaper to pull it down than repair it. That was the norm. It is easy with hindsight to criticise, and it must be remembered that Hoyland was not destroyed maliciously but with the best intentions, when it was decided to spend as much as possible on development before the local government changes took place in 1974. It was generally believed locally that Hoyland had little prospect of money being invested in its facilities once Hoyland UDC had ceased to look after its affairs. That concern has proved largely true. Unfortunately, the plans for Hoyland's transformation backfired. In the haste that followed the decision to redevelop Hoyland, the baby was thrown out with the bath water. Conservation and restoration would have been the best solution but the majority of Hoyland's finest buildings were destroyed; much of central Hoyland now looks like a bomb site. The intended redevelopment did not come to full fruition, and today there are gaping spaces where buildings once stood. Even the old commercial properties which remain are largely disfigured by uninspired, unsympathetic, modern shop-fronts. The closure of coal mines and supporting industries has created a void in local employment prospects, mirroring what happened when Elsecar Ironworks and Milton Ironworks closed a century previously. The recovery this time has been slow. Mass unemployment, particularly among young people, has brought a whole series of social problems. Vandalism, arson attacks and general lawlessness have added to the decline of Hoyland. When business has finished for the day, shop windows and doors are covered with ugly metal shutters. Hoyland town centre used to be a bustling place all through the week. In comparison, Hoyland is now like a ghost town. At the weekend the streets are busier at night-time, when groups of young revellers visit the town centre pubs. By 10 o'clock High Street, King Street, Milton Road and Market Street are busy with young people – but the trend in the last twenty years to 'modernise' Hoyland's public houses has taken away virtually every vestige of the traditional pub.

Hoyland War Memorial and Longfields Crescent, 1920s. *(Walker's Newsagents collection)*

Auction of property owned by the late George Dawes. *(Joan Hopson collection)*

Methodism was introduced to Hoyland by John Johnson of Thorpe Hesley. Mr Johnson came to live at Manor Farm in about 1747, after which Methodist preachers often stayed there. John Wesley preached from the Tithe Lane steps in Hoyland in 1772. Interest in Methodism grew and in 1809 Hoyland Wesleyan chapel was constructed at a cost of £800 on a central site, on land donated by William Gray, the then occupant of Manor House Farm. This photograph of about 1880 shows the chapel shortly before the entrance was altered. Compare this photograph with the one on page 4, which shows the building after the alterations. The Wesleyan chapel has been known at St Paul's since 1932, when the various Methodist sects in Hoyland amalgamated. Several other chapels were also re-named at this time. The last service at St Paul's was held in May 1975, after which the congregation moved to the newly converted Thistle House, former home and surgery of Dr Barclay Wiggins, situated between Duke Street and Tithe Lane, further along Market Street. Since 1977 St Paul's has been occupied by Charisma Antiques, run by John Simmons and his wife and business partner, Christine. (*Frank Kelly collection*)

High Street, looking towards Post Office Buildings at the top of Milton Road, seen in the background, early 1900s. The building on the left, before the old Gardeners Arms, which later became Beatties Busy Corner, is occupied by Moses Fletcher, confectioner. Herbert Garner's ironmonger's shop, with its large bay window which extends almost into the road, at 22 High Street, is opposite. The space between Garners and Holly House, whose garden wall can be seen emerging from the side of the house into High Street, was filled by the John Knowles Memorial Church. (*Frank Kelly collection*)

The Princess Theatre, West Street, *c. 1895*. It was built by the Hoyland firm John Parr and Sons and opened on Boxing Day 1893, with Lawrence Daly's company in a performance of *Cissie*. The theatre was packed and hundreds were turned away. It specialised in melodrama, a popular form of entertainment at that time, and many professional touring theatre companies played there. Its first owner was William Ottley, who until his death in 1914 was the proprietor of the drapery and millinery shop in King Street, which continued to be run by his widow. Ottley's old shop is presently occupied by Thawley's Newsagents. In addition to 'legitimate' theatre productions such as *The Corsican Brothers*, *The Sign of the Cross*, and *The Bells*, variety shows were staged there. A comedian from one of these shows married the widowed landlady of the Queen's Head. Local amateurs also appeared there; one of them, Roy Colville, was a photographer. He played many leading roles in the productions staged at the theatre. Prices ranged from 15s for a box or 3s 6d for a single seat; a seat in the balcony cost 2s. For a seat in the pit stalls the price was 1s 6d; the pit cost 9d and the gallery 6d. By 1902 silent films were often shown between the acts of plays, and by the 1920s live shows were no longer a feature, the Princess's interior having been altered to increase the size of the auditorium and adapted to become a fully fledged picture palace. In the book *Curtains!!! or A New Life for Old Theatres* Christopher Brereton lists the theatre as the Empire Hippodrome (formerly Princess Theatre); exactly when that name was used I have been unable to ascertain, but for most of its life since the 1920s the theatre has been known by the Americanised-German name Kino. The Kino has not shown films for the last forty years: it has been providing an entirely different kind of entertainment, operating as a bingo hall. The name Princess Theatre is still proudly emblazoned in stone on its front gable. Hoyland is fortunate that it can boast an actual theatre building within its boundaries, something that even many large towns in England cannot. *(Frank Kelly collection)*

King Street, *c.* 1905. In the right foreground is John Guest and Sons Ltd, pawnbrokers and clothiers, above which is the old Queen's Head. Victoria Street goes off to the right and the entrance to Sebastopol is on the left, opposite the Queen's Head. The landlord of this popular pub (which was replaced by a new building, set back, and opened just before the Second World War) was John J. Dewhirst. He died in 1905 and his widow Charlotte kept the licence until 1933. They had two sons, Mark and Reg. Mark ran a grocery business from the shop on the corner of Victoria Street, after which he worked at Hoyland cinema. The shop was run by Edwin Thompson at the time of this photograph. It was last occupied as a dry cleaner's before being demolished in October 1968. Reg Dewhirst was originally a colliery electrician. He ended his working life running a grocery and confectionery shop. The premises which he later occupied can be seen on the left. He retired in the early 1970s, after which he and his wife Elsie moved to Hall Street. The landlady of the Queen's Head, Mrs Charlotte Dewhirst, re-married. Her husband was a comedian, Fred Titcombe, whom she met after he appeared in a variety show at the Princess Theatre. The Primitive Methodist chapel, whose pediment can be seen on the left, was built in 1880. The building of the New Connexion chapel, whose pediment can be seen on the right, followed a year later. This chapel was built in front of a smaller chapel, erected in 1860, which on the opening of the new chapel became redundant and later was used as a schoolroom. Above the New Connexion chapel is the Five Alls, a pub which closed at about the same time as the new Queen's Head opened, after which it became a private house. The building was demolished in 1973. Guest's former shop ended its days as Derek Bean's antiques shop, before being demolished in the 1960s. (*Frank Kelly collection*)

The right-hand side of part of King Street, *c.* 1900. William Joll stands outside his greengrocer's shop. The buildings between Joll's and the Co-operative grocery store were not trading premises at that time. The gap in the buildings was filled a few years later with a shop which was occupied by William Joll's son Ernest, who opened a china shop. It later became Davies' Boot Repairers and is currently the Abbey Veterinary Clinic. From the 1940s Madge Hastie was running her ladies' hairdresser's shop, next door to Davies, taken over by Florence Roberts in the 1950s. She ran a wool shop at the front of the premises and Florence's hairdressing salon at the rear into the 1980s. Next door was Hastie's butcher's shop, which had been run by Henry Vincent Hastie until his death in 1932. His son Reginald followed him in the business. Above Hastie's was Clayton's shoe shop, formerly the premises of William Joll. In recent years the premises occupied by Joll's and Hastie's has become Cook's, decorating and DIY shop; and Florence's former hairdressing salon is now Franklyn's take-away. Florence Robert's daughter Lynda carried on her mother's business, moving to a shop in Market Street in the group of buildings adjacent to Little Leeds. *(Frank Kelly collection)*

This view of Hoyland Town Hall, *c.* 1903, shows the newly positioned horse trough, erected to celebrate the reign of Queen Victoria and the coronation of Edward VII. The stones of the clocktower, added in 1892 to provide another amenity, thanks to the benevolence of businesswoman Martha Knowles, are mellowing and acquiring the sooty grime characteristic of the rest of the structure. The Knowles's business premises on the corner of Market Street and King Street were later taken over by Ward's and then by the long-established Hoyland business Rowland Cross & Son, opened in 1789. *(Doreen Howse collection)*

The top of King Street, *c.* 1905. The railings on the right mark the corner of Hoyland Town Hall at the junction of George Street, High Street, King Street and Market Street. A new sign displaying the name Matthew has been erected above the doorway of 1 King Street, after the death of the former proprietor Joseph Willey, chemist and dentist, in 1903. This is the building with the name George Street emblazoned on its side. J.E. Matthew was in business as a chemist at 26 King Street and 41 Church Street, Elsecar, at this time. The Globe Tea Company later occupied this shop, until its demolition in November 1970. *(Frank Kelly collection)*

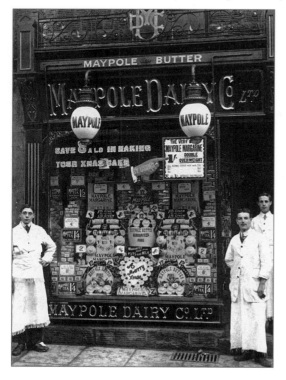

No. 28 King Street, occupied by the Maypole Dairy Co. Ltd, 1912. The manager, Albert Reynolds, who ran the Maypole until he retired to Skegness during the Second World War, stands in the right foreground. This was one of Hoyland's superior purveyors of comestibles for almost sixty years. As can be seen, its shop-front was impressively appointed, with the lettering picked out in gold. The interior was fitted out in an equally superior fashion with a marble floor and tiled walls, with the company's emblem, featuring a maypole with figures dancing around it, prominently displayed. The Maypole specialised in dairy products and traded until 1971. *(Author's collection)*

Hoyland Law takes its name from the Anglo-Saxon word 'hlaew', which simply means hill. It is the highest point in Hoyland, rising to almost 600 ft. Hoyland Law is in fact the highest point from Hoyland to the east coast. In many publications it is implied that Hoyland Law Stand was built by the Townend family. They may well have used it as a hunting lodge at some time, but during his extensive research Arthur K. Clayton discovered the truth. On the instructions of that most prolific of builders of monuments, the Marquess of Rockingham, a tower was built on Hoyland Law in 1750. This photograph was taken in the early 1900s and shows Hoyland Law Stand while it was being used as a private residence. After the Dearne Valley Water Board took over the surrounding site the Law Stand was abandoned. *(George Hardy collection)*

Hoyland Law Stand, 17 July 1999. This shows just how much the structure has deteriorated during more than half a century of neglect. Since the site is no longer required by Yorkshire Water, the Marquess of Rockingham's tower is up for sale. It is hoped locally that the buyer will restore it and put it to good use. *(Author's commission)*

Earl Fitzwilliam's Milton Pottery was situated at Skiers Spring, near the brickworks. It operated from 1911 until 1931 and specialised in the production of pancheons, bread pots, plant pots and utilitarian household items. Two brothers named Keir came from Cumbria to run the pottery. As well as producing items for export outside the area, goods were made to order for anyone who made a personal call at the works. Hoyland's newest pub, the Potters Wheel on the Cloughs Estate, was named to commemorate Milton Pottery. *(Chris Thawley collection)*

The Strafford Arms and Hoyland Cinema House, early 1920s (see also page 29). *(Joan Hopson collection)*

Hall's original shop at 35 King Street, *c.* 1914. George Hall was a potato merchant who branched out and became a greengrocer and fruiterer. He and his wife Edna had sixteen children, many of whom set up greengrocery businesses themselves. There were Hall's shops in Hoyland, Elsecar and Hoyland Common, as well as mobile concerns. The two older girls on the doorstep are the Misses Doreen and Edna Hall. It is interesting to see the wide range of goods on display. Various members of the Hall family continued to trade from the premises until the 1970s, when on the retirement of Mrs Kate Marsden, George and Edna's granddaughter, the business closed. Hall's still have businesses in Hoyland today. Jack Hall and his sons John and Frank have greengrocer's shops in High Street, in one half of the downstairs portion of Storey and Cooper's old shop, and a shop unit at the top of Hoyland Market, as well as trading at Penistone Market. The Hall family also own the florist's shop Cottage Flowers in Market Street, situated in the single-storey, double-fronted stone building next to Harvey and Richardson. This shop had been a hairdresser's during the 1980s before which it was Derek Bean's antiques shop. George Thomas also traded from there during the 1950s and 1960s. He sold a variety of goods during the time he ran his business, often changing his lines. He also had an ice cream-making business and Thomas's ice cream van used to do its rounds throughout the locality. For many years before George Thomas took over, the shop had been a tobacconist's. *(George Hardy collection)*

High Street, *c.* 1920. The John Knowles Memorial Church was built in the gap between Herbert Garner's ironmonger's shop and Holly House. The church was built after the new Vicar of St Peter's, the Rev. Charles William Bennett, placed a brass cross and two candlesticks on the altar. These items were a gift from the parishioners of the church he had previously served as curate. The parishioners of the then chapel of ease, St Andrew's, were outraged at what they considered to be papist leanings. One of them, Mrs Elizabeth Bartlett, the only daughter of Martha Knowles, was so incensed that she erected at her own expense a new church for the Free Church of England, and named it in memory of her brother, who had died at the age of 52 in 1899. Two foundation stones were laid on 20 September 1911, by Elizabeth Bartlett and the Right Rev. William Troughton, Bishop Primus of the Free Church of England. All the buildings seen in this view remain today, including Holly House. In 1927 Holly House was purchased from the Firth family (the well-known elocution and drama teacher Miss Florence D. Firth lived at Holly House as a child, until it was sold) by Mr and Mrs Harry Cooper and two double-fronted shops were built on to its front. Mrs Cooper and her sister Mrs Storey had been running a drapery business in a small shop in King Street since just after the First World War. They moved into the two-storey shop next to the church and traded as Storey & Cooper. The other shop was rented to Melias, a grocery firm. The stones of Holly House can be clearly seen attached to the red bricks of the extension, if one follows the line of the wall at the side of the present pet shop. (*Frank Kelly collection*)

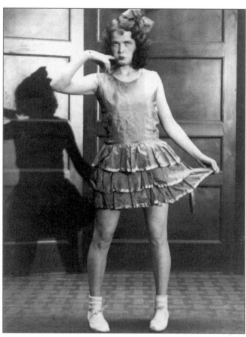

During the 1920s and '30s, after live acts stopped appearing at the Princess Theatre, there was no stage in the area other than at the Strafford Arms. Acts used to appear on the small stage in the Concert Room and people came from miles around to see them. The landlord at this time was Reginald Hinton, and during his tenure Hoyland's largest and most prestigious pub was nicknamed the Leg and Tit, a name by which some of Hoyland's older residents still refer to it. During the early 19th century it was called The Beggar and Gentleman but that name was short lived, and it was decided to name it the Strafford Arms, in honour of the great Earl of Strafford (1593–1641), who lived at Wentworth Woodhouse. These four photographs show some of the acts on the stage at the Strafford Arms. *(Joan Hopson collection)*

It seems unbelievable that one of England's greatest historical figures should not continue to be commemorated in the name of a public house situated so close to his home, in an area the greater part of which was owned by his family for centuries. The Strafford Arms was renamed The Beggar and The Gentleman (note the addition of another 'the') in the mid-1980s. In 1999 the pub sign reads Beggar and Gentleman. It has twice been refurbished since the 1970s. All the rooms which once provided a refuge for different groups of locals have been knocked into one. Here are four more photographs of the acts appearing on the stage at the Strafford Arms. *(Joan Hopson collection)*

A large number of the photographs which appear in this book are from a collection belonging to Walker's Newsagents, one of Hoyland's oldest surviving businesses. The first of the Walkers to trade in Hoyland was Isaac Lichmere, a keen amateur photographer. Many of the photographs reproduced here were taken by him. He also commissioned Roy Colville to take views of the area. Roy Colville's studio at West Bank was taken over by Alf Hoyland and is now run by Alf's daughter Vicky. The Colville photographs were turned into postcards published by I.L. Walker. Walker's have been established in Hoyland since the early part of the reign of George V. The family had been in the wholesale and retail newsagency business since the 1880s when John Robert Walker (1860–1929) was trading from a shop in Grahams Orchard in Barnsley. John Robert was a younger son of Isaac Walker, an edge tool maker of Masbrough, Rotherham. This photograph shows the Walker family outside the Fountain Inn, *c.* 1893. Mrs Lydia Walker sits beside her husband and in the back of the trap are two of their children, Isaac Lichmere and Nelly. (*Walker's Newsagents collection*)

Walker's original shop in Grahams Orchard, Barnsley, *c.* 1895. (*Walker's Newsagents collection*)

Walker's shop at 8 King Street, *c.* 1930. The front of the shop has been signwritten with the name L. Walker. As everyone knew him as Lichie, perhaps he thought it was better to drop the I (for Isaac).

Isaac Lichmere Walker (1885–1958) married Annetta Crowe (1886–1959) in Wombwell on 31 October 1911. Miss Crowe's parents kept the Corner Pin in Barnsley. After working alongside his father, 'Lichie' Walker, as he was invariably known, started in business on his own as a confectioner. His speciality was toffee. His son, Geoffrey, was born on 11 May 1914 in Hoyland, where Lichie and 'Netta', as Mrs Walker was known, had become established. Young Geoff went to Market Street School before attending Barnsley Grammar School. By the early 1920s Walker's were trading from 8 King Street in the newsagency and stationery business, at premises from which Lloyd's had traded as newsagents in the early 1900s: they had been bought by Lichie Walker's aunt, Mrs Rothwell. Lichie took over the newsagency and continued to make toffee at the back of his shop. At that time Walker's had the exclusive rights to sell the *News of the World* in Hoyland. The Walkers lived at the house known as Windyridge in Upper Hoyland, until they moved briefly to 73 Longfields Crescent until the house they had built and named Arrandale, in West Street, was completed. After the deaths of Lichie and Netta, Arrandale became the residence of their daughter Joan. Joan Walker was born in 1916 and married an RAF pilot Fred Fletcher, who was shot down over Holland on his return from a bombing mission to Germany. She later married Benjamin Clarke, and opened a newsagency with her husband in Royston. They later moved to Grimsby and opened another newsagent's. Joan and Benny Clarke returned to Hoyland in 1959, having sold their business and for a time helped out at Walker's shop. Then Benny took a light job as a general handyman for Lord Fitzwilliam at Wentworth Woodhouse. In this view of King Street and High Street in the early 1920s Walker's shop can be seen next door to Ottley's on the right. *(Walker's Newsagents collection)*

On 17 May 1932 Herbert Garner, the ironmonger, died suddenly. Lichie Walker saw an opportunity to expand into larger premises. Exactly how long it took for the business to transfer from King Street to High Street is not clear, because receipts and bills on file show 8 King Street as late as 1935. The first bill addressed to Walkers at 22 High Street is in 1936. When Douglas Porteous Beattie retired and Beatties Busy Corner closed down, shortly before the Second World War, his bus and railway agencies were taken over by Walker's. This is High Street, 1936. Lichie Walker has settled into his new premises at 22 High Street. Note the big sign above the bay window. Beyond the John Knowles Memorial Church, the distinctive signs of Storey and Cooper and Melias can be seen. (*Walker's Newsagents collection*)

High Street, early 1960s. On the left is 13 High Street, which was at that time occupied by the Labour Exchange, having formerly been Beatties Busy Corner and before that Moses Fletcher's Old Eccles Cake Shop. The distinctive John Smith's Brewery inn sign can be seen beyond the Rover; it is on the forecourt of the Gardener's Arms. In the distance are Post Office Buildings: Alfred Ellaway's newsagent's at 1 Milton Road can be seen on the left of May Taylor's ladies' and children's outfitters. Ellaway's was taken over by Brian Dixon a few years after this photograph was taken; he moved his shop to Ottley's old shop in King Street, shortly before his former shop was razed to the ground in the early 1970s. Dixon's newsagent's was taken over by Adrian and Wendy Thawley, on Brian Dixon's retirement during the last decade. The gable end displaying the Oakwell Ales sign belongs to Higgs's off-licence. Walker's new shop-front can be seen with its blind down, next door to which is Claude Ellstone's, a shop which David Walker would take over in the decade that followed. (*Walker's Newsagents collection*)

Walker's shop at 22 High Street, 1955. The big bay window, a feature of Garner's old shop, has been replaced with the flat shop-front seen here. This front was replaced shortly after this photograph was taken by a tiled front with the name Walker's in large 3D chrome letters above the two windows and central doorway; that front has been superseded by yet another tiled front that extends across no. 24, which David Walker acquired when Claude Ellstone's confectioner's and tobacconist's closed in 1974. Until 1997 Walker's used no. 24 as a gardening shop during the spring and summer, sold fireworks from it in the autumn, then cards and decorations in the lead-up to Christmas. The dividing wall was knocked through in the most recent redevelopment of the present-day air-conditioned shop, and the new shop-front has a re-positioned double entrance door. In the photograph Geoff Walker (1914–95), who joined Lichie in the family business after working for a time as an electrician at Rockingham Colliery, helps his father unload a parcel from the back of their Bedford delivery van, which also doubled as the family's car. Two of the assistants are carrying magazines. On the left is Gwennie Taylor (now Mrs Emson) and on the right Joan Wright. Geoff Walker married Avice Hague (1914–94) at St Andrew's parish church, Hoyland, on 1 January 1940. Avice was a telephonist at Hoyland Telephone Exchange, where her parents, Arthur and Ada, were caretakers. Geoff and Avice lived at The Nook, in West Street, opposite Hoyland war memorial. Their sons Ralph and David grew up there. Geoff and Avice moved to a bungalow in George Street in 1977, which had previously been occupied by Mr and Mrs Derek Clough and their daughter Brenda. Mr Clough was a builder and Mrs Clough ran the DIY shop at the top of Milton, which moved to virtually the same site as Lichie Walker's original shop when the new buildings were constructed in 1972. The actual site of 8 King Street is now a gap, which allows access to the maisonettes above the parade of shops. Clough's DIY shop closed and was later occupied by Binn's baker's, and the Cloughs moved out of the district. In the lead-up to the redevelopment of Hoyland town centre in 1971 another newsagent, who had a long-established business in King Street, Maurice Layte, decided to retire. Walker's bought the business and incorporated it into their own; Layte's shop was demolished, and Barclays Bank now occupies the site. Walker's continues to be run by David Walker (younger son of Geoff) and his wife Christine, ably assisted by their numerous staff. (*Walker's Newsagents collection*)

Hoyland Hall, *c.* 1920. This is arguably the finest of the few remaining Georgian buildings in Hoyland, and for almost 200 years it was the township's principal residence. Exactly for whom Hoyland Hall was built is not currently known, and it may have been built on the site of an earlier hall, as Hoyland Hall is mentioned in documents dating back to 1579. The hall seen here was used as a residence for various high-ranking officials connected with the iron industry. Henry Hartop, a partner in the Milton Ironworks who later ran Elsecar Ironworks for Lord Fitzwilliam, was resident here from the early 1820s until 1841, as was William Vizard, the first owner of Hoyland Silkstone Colliery. It later served as the residence for various managers of the colliery until the 1920s, and after closure of the mine the managers of Rockingham Colliery lived there. Its architect is unknown but it may well have been designed by John Carr who, in addition to carrying out work of the first rank at Wentworth Woodhouse and both major and minor commissions on the Wentworth Estate, was also responsible for building several smaller gentlemen's residences in the area, including New Lodge, near Barnsley. Another possible architect is John Platt II. Although Hoyland Hall is not listed in the records which survive of the commissions he received, he is a strong contender because of the style and scale of the building. He worked extensively in the area and built Thundercliffe Grange for the Earl of Effingham and carried out work at Wortley Hall and Wentworth Castle, as well as building at least one house in Wentworth. After Hoyland Hall ceased to be a private residence it was used for educational purposes for over twenty years. During the 1980s it was boarded up and remained empty, and was broken into and stripped of some of its chimney-pieces and fittings. Its future seemed uncertain, but a buyer was found. Hoyland Hall was extended in the early 1990s and now forms the nucleus of an old people's home. The new building has been constructed in a style and in building materials which complement the Georgian hall. Unfortunately the small walled park which surrounds it has not received such sympathetic treatment. (*Walker's Newsagents collection*)

St Helen's Catholic church, West Street, c. 1930. The building of the Dearne and Dove Canal and later the railway, which brought Irish labourers or navvies to Hoyland, resulted in an influx of Catholics to Hoyland and district. Many married local girls and settled in the area. Less than seventy years later, there were enough Catholics living there to warrant building a place of worship. The first Catholic church was built in Elsecar in 1866 and dedicated to St Helen, mother of the Roman Emperor Constantine. Built of dressed sandstone it had a high pitched roof. In its lifetime it served a number of useful purposes, being variously a school, the Midland Working Men's Club and the Hoyland office of the DHSS. The presbytery was originally Prospect House, which stands next to the Clothier's Arms. The wooden-framed bungalow built at the top of Hill Street replaced it. In the 1890s the church and the new presbytery was purchased by the Midland Railway Company, who drove their railway line between the church and Cobcar Street. The church was demolished within the last decade; the site is now occupied by several small houses. In the 1890s church officials bought a site in West Street, where a small cemetery was consecrated and a school and presbytery built. Whereas before lessons had been given in the church, mass was now celebrated in a schoolroom; it is the part of the school building to the left of the church. The new church was eventually built in the Italian Tuscan style and consecrated in 1929. A small Catholic Working Men's Club was built near the presbytery. In the early 1970s this was replaced by a larger club, which has a large hall above, used for functions and events connected with the church. (*Walker's Newsagents collection*)

Edward B. Masheder moved from Tankersley Lane to run Milton Motor Co. in 1948. This garage stood at the top of Milton Road on part of the site of the present Kwik-Save, facing the Ball Inn. The original garage and vehicle repair shop occupied the buildings to the right of the photograph, which had been George Fleetwood's blacksmith's shop until his retirement. Masheder's took over the middle portion in the 1950s, this having previously belonged to the Hoyland building firm J. Parr and Sons, was adapted to form the garage shown in the photograph. Joan, Ted's wife, joined him in the running of the business and the Masheders became a prominent couple in the life of Hoyland's business community. Their mechanic Maurice Jones is still well known around the district. Ted Masheder was a keen amateur photographer, and captured on film many views of old Hoyland and the demolition that destroyed the heart of Hoyland in the early 1970s. In 1972 the premises of the Milton Motor Co. were compulsorily purchased by Hoyland UDC, as part of their town centre redevelopment programme. They later compulsorily purchased the garden belonging to Masheder's bungalow in two further stages, which reduced Masheder's plot by over two thirds. Southgate was constructed on the site. (*Joan Masheder collection*)

King Street, *c. 1958*. On the left-hand side is the Barnsley British Co-operative Society's grocery store. Out of sight is Davies', shoe repairers, then Florence's, Hastie's and Clayton's shoe shop. On the right is the Co-op Chemists, on the other corner of Booth Street is Bradley's Shop, which sold a whole range of items, from hardware to toys and fancy goods, Bolton's the Bakers, Salter's butcher's, the Maypole, Parkin's living quarters (presently the Everest Indian takeaway), Parkin's chemist's, the Co-op butcher's and the Co-op drapery store, above which can be seen the detached house belonging to Mr George and Mrs Mabel Hoyland. Mrs Hoyland was the former Miss Ottley, and the shop which she continued to run on the death of her mother as Ottley's is next door. The buildings from Bradley's as far as Parkin's living quarters were demolished in the mid-1970s. *(George Hardy collection)*

King Street and High Street, *c. 1958*. On the left is the Turf Tavern. It was owned by Samuel Smith's Tadcaster Brewery and was licensed to sell beer, ale and porter but not wines and spirits, and closed in 1960 when the Turf pub was built on part of the garden of Greenfield House, the former home of Martha Knowles. This new pub was later called The Kestrel, in honour of local author Barry Hines, whose highly acclaimed novel *A Kestrel for a Knave* was made into the equally highly acclaimed film *Kes*. The Kestrel was recently demolished. Beyond the Turf

Tavern is Layte's newsagent's, then Clayton's furniture shop, Tal Lowbridge's barber's shop and the Globe Tea Company. On the right can be seen the corner of Ottley's shop, then Don Valley Cleaners at 8 King Street, E. Norwood, opticians, and Maltby's greengrocer's. Mrs Alice Ann Maltby was the former Miss Hall; Maltby's was run by her children Bessie and Vic, who moved into a new shop on the site in 1972. That shop is now run by Eaden's. Beyond Maltby's is Rowland's Cross shop and in High Street can be seen Ellstone's, Walker's, the John Knowles Memorial Church, Storey and Cooper, Melias and the gable end of Higgs's shop. *(George Hardy collection)*

Town Hall, *c.* 1960. In the foreground can be seen the bonnet of Geoff Walker's Morris shooting brake. Compare this view of the Town Hall with that on page 12. The horse trough and steps seen in that photograph were removed in the 1920s when the balustrade was added, closing off the front entrance. Access was gained by the steps seen leading to the door on the right. Hoyland Town Hall closed on 11 June 1973 and was demolished almost immediately. A new Town Hall, situated above a newly constructed Co-operative grocery store and freezer centre, had already been built around it. The entrance to the new Town Hall was turned 180 degrees from the original entrance of the Town Hall seen here. (*Edward Ellis collection*)

High Street from Milton Road, 1960. The photographs shows Guest's butcher's, Higgs's fish and chip shop, Higgs's off-licence, and Storey and Cooper beyond. (*Joan Masheder collection*)

The Strafford Arms Basket Room, 1964, shortly after landlord George A. Hopson and his wife Joan, seen here, took it over. *(Joan Hopson collection)*

The Strafford Arms in 1965, shortly after the old Basket Room had been refurbished. The panelling and the fireplace are the only features of the much missed Strafford, that are recognisable in the present public house. The Concert Room, Blue Room and Public Bar or Tap Room have gone. The exterior of the pub now called Beggar and Gentleman, or by many simply as t' Beggar, remains substantially unaltered. *(Joan Hopson collection)*

This is a visit to Harlow in Essex by Hoyland shopkeepers and businessmen, who as members of Hoyland Chamber of Trade formed a property development company to work with Hoyland Nether UDC to help redevelop Hoyland town centre. This fact-finding mission was to view the various facilities provided in Harlow, in the shopping areas and at sports centres. Members of the council were guests of Hoyland Chamber of Trade. In the photograph are Frank Perrin, optician, Len Kennworthy, coach proprietor, Cllr Arthur Loy, Cllr Dennis Eaden, Cllr Jack Ashmore, Brian Hoggard, Housing Manager, Dennis Roberts, Town Clerk, Cllr Minnie Gillis (partially hidden), Frank Vickers, proprietor of Storey and Cooper, and David Walker, newsagent and Secretary of Hoyland Chamber of Trade. Also present was Ted Masheder of the Milton Motor Co., the photographer. *(Joan Masheder collection)*

A view in 1971 from the site once occupied by Mount Tabor chapel (formerly the Primitive Methodist chapel) across King Street to C. Firth and Sons at no. 46, which was built in 1907. After the last of the Firths retired the shop became Hepworth's for a brief period before being taken over by Doreen Law, who sells wool, haberdashery and ladies' and children's wear. Peter's barber's shop and the Vanity Box, ladies' hairdressers, are below. Across Bethel Street can be seen the gable end of the former Five Alls public house. *(Joan Masheder collection)*

From the bottom of Milton towards Hoyland, early 1970s. The Furnace Inn, a public house owned by the famous Sheffield brewery Ward's, can be seen on the left. Along with another famous brewery, Vaux, of Newcastle-upon-Tyne, Ward's brewery was closed by the group which then owned both breweries in June 1999. *(Joan Masheder collection)*

Hoyland Cinema House, 1970. The once-impressive building, which by that time had been standing empty for over twenty years, was looking very run down indeed. It was demolished the following year. *(Joan Masheder collection)*

Hoyland used to have Christmas decorations throughout the town centre. The Christmas tree was usually positioned near the Strafford Arms, as shown here in 1970, where Hoyland Silver Prize Band used to practise in the Concert Room every Friday evening. The band would hold open-air concerts around the tree, which were greatly appreciated. In recent years at Christmas time Hoyland's streets have sadly had nothing to denote the season of goodwill. (*Joan Masheder collection*)

Hoyland Market laid out at the back of the Town Hall on its temporary site, October 1970. Hoyland police station (built 1889, demolished 1972) can be seen in George Street. Every building in this photograph was razed to the ground within less than two years. Encouraged by Hoyland Nether UDC, a London-based firm, the Grasim Group of Companies, re-opened Hoyland Market on 24 October 1970. Barnsley Council tried to invoke a charter forbidding anyone from opening a market within a 7 mile radius of Barnsley, but they were on to a non-starter as the precedent had already been made by Hoyland's former market. Within less than two years the market was moved back to the site of the original, opening on 10 June 1972 under the control of Hoyland UDC. A new police station was built at Hoyland Common. (*Joan Masheder collection*)

High Street in 1970, shortly before redevelopment work commenced. An advertising sign for Hoyland Trade Fair, taking place between 27 and 29 October at the Milton Hall, Elsecar, is being displayed across Roland Cross and Son's shop, which is standing empty. *(Joan Masheder collection)*

A view of the distinctive gable of a house in Victoria Street occupied by the Hyde family, taken from Bethel Street after the clearance of properties had taken place. The tin roof of Barber Street Working Men's Club can be seen to the left. *(Joan Masheder collection)*

A view of the corner of Post Office Buildings and West Street, 1970. Amongst the shops on the left can be seen Ben Sorby's fishmonger's and Jack Hall's fruit and vegetable shop. On the right, the former gas showrooms, one-time Mell's joiners and undertakers, is being occupied by Taylor's electrical shop, above which Gallon's Stores are standing empty. Gallon's Stores and all the shops on the left were demolished. *(Joan Masheder collection)*

The greengrocer's shop known as Covent Garden, which was situated next to the Turf Tavern, can be seen on the left. Across the road, Mabel Hoyland (the former Miss Ottley) has retired, and has let her shop to Bennett's, who were running a small supermarket and butcher's shop when this photograph was taken in 1970. *(Joan Masheder collection)*

The magnificent view, dating from 1971 but unchanged today, from Millmount Road across Elsecar reservoir to Wentworth. The distinctive spire of Wentworth Church dominates the skyline. Millmount Road and the new houses seen here, built by the Elsecar firm of W. Chadwick and Son, occupy the site of Sebastopol (pronounced Sebastapool locally), which had once formed part of the estate of George Dawes, built to accommodate workers from the Milton Ironworks. The ironworks were situated to the right of the large field (out of view), now known as the 'Forge', seen in the centre of the photograph. Sebastopol was cleared in the 1950s. *(Joan Masheder collection)*

High Street, November 1971. Demolition in Hoyland town centre has commenced. Roland's Cross shop has been partly dismantled and work is being carried out in King Street. *(Joan Masheder collection)*

Maltby's shop. The date-stone above the doorway is inscribed G B 1804. The demolition of these late Georgian buildings was unnecessary, but apparently, as the song goes, 'it seemed like a good idea at the time'. *(Joan Masheder collection)*

Above the King Street entrance of Roland Cross and Son can be seen the date-stone with R H 1814 inscribed on it. Below, the bulldozer wreaks havoc on Maltby's old shop. *(Joan Masheder collection)*

The bulldozer positions itself before the façade of Maltby's shop. Lichie Walker's old shop at no. 8 has been almost finished off. *(Joan Masheder collection)*

Gone in a cloud of dust, 167 years of history! *(Joan Masheder collection)*

After the clearance of the buildings above Layte's and Clayton's, including Harold Oxspring Lowbridge's shop (Tal Lowbridge) and the Globe Tea Company, in November 1970, the former original early 19th-century Primitive Methodist chapel was revealed. The chapel had been converted into two shops in the early years of the 20th century. As can be seen from the next view, it was once a fine building. *(Joan Masheder collection)*

A side and rear view of the former Primitive Methodist chapel, King Street, November 1970. *(Joan Masheder collection)*

The whole corner site of Market Street and King Street after its late Georgian buildings had been razed to the ground. The site was photographed in 1971, shortly before building of the modern shops and maisonettes commenced. *(Joan Masheder collection)*

The entire site of the upper part of King Street had been cleared by early 1971. *(Joan Masheder collection)*

Hoyland's new Town Hall from High Street, July 1999. The large windows on the second floor above the Co-operative Pioneer supermarket are for the former Council Chamber of Hoyland Nether UDC. The supermarket and new Town Hall were built using extremely expensive handmade bricks, and were ready for occupation in June 1973. This building was constructed around Hoyland's much-missed Town Hall of 1840. The ground-floor portion of the building to the right was originally the Co-op Freezer Centre. That venture was short lived. The large plate glass windows were bricked up and painted, and the Freezer Centre was incorporated into the supermarket. It is amazing that in the 1960s there were so many different Co-op shops in Hoyland: grocery, butchers, chemists, shoes, hardware and drapery as well as other Co-ops in Hoyland Common and Elsecar. Yet today there is just one supermarket. So much for redevelopment.

   Below: the entrance of Hoyland's new Town Hall seen from Southgate, 1999. *(Author's commission)*

Looking up King Street towards High Street by night, between 10.15 pm and 10.30 pm on 21 July 1999. The modern buildings which replaced the late Georgian Primitive Methodist chapel and the parade of early 19th-century shops can be seen on the left. The gap between Thawley's Newsagents and the new buildings on the right was the site of Lichie Walker's King Street shop. *(Author's commission)*

A view of High Street by night, between 10.15 and 10.30 pm on 21 July 1999. Until recently shops used to have their windows lighted until 10 o'clock. Walker's, with its new shop-front seen here, were noted for their interesting and attractive window displays. At Christmas time, Valentine's Day and Halloween the windows provided passers-by with something interesting to look at. Hoyland in the 1980s and 1990s became a very different place. Shopkeepers could no longer afford to insure their plate glass windows, which sometimes didn't last more than a week. They were left with no alternative but to fit protective metal shutters. *(Author's commission)*

Hoyland's boundary at the beginning of Hoyland Common, 1970. The signpost to the left proclaims that you are entering the Urban District of Hoyland Nether. The building on the right is the Cross Keys public house. *(Joan Masheder collection)*

Hoyland Common Junior School, winter 1970. *(Joan Masheder collection)*

Allotts Corner, *c.* 1880. Tankersley Lane can be seen beyond. *(Chris Thawley collection)*

A policeman directing traffic at Allotts Corner, Hoyland Common, *c.* 1920. Allott's were high-class bakers and confectioners. Even though Allott's themselves have not been trading in Hoyland Common for over thirty years, people still ask for Allott's Corner when travelling by bus from Sheffield or Barnsley. *(Chris Thawley collection)*

Allott's rather splendid delivery dray, *c.* 1900. *(Chris Thawley collection)*

Looking towards St Peter's Church from the bottom of Hawshaw Lane at its junction with Fearnley Road, Hoyland Common, 1970. *(Joan Masheder collection)*

CHAPTER TWO

ELSECAR

The place-name Elsecar is unique. Else or Ellsi was a Saxon lord, who is known to have owned land in the area. The word car often appears in place-names of ancient British settlements. The two names combined suggest that a settlement, albeit a small one, existed in Saxon times. Another possible explanation for the name is that it means Elsi's marsh: car is an old name for low, swampy ground and Elsecar lies in a valley, which may well have been a marsh centuries ago. Within Elsecar is the area known as Cobcar. This may be a form of the Scandinavian word for hill, 'kop'. For centuries Elsecar was nothing more than a series of scattered farms and cottages, growing into a village proper some time after the second decade of the 18th century, when the Watson-Wentworth family of Wentworth Woodhouse began to develop the mineral resources in the area. Industrial buildings appeared in the Elsecar valley, and cottages and houses were built to accommodate the increasing population. By the end of the century a thriving community had been established. Coal mining began under the Low Wood early in the century, and by 1750 Elsecar Old Colliery had been sunk. This pit had its main shaft on Elsecar Green, situated where the Market Hall was later built, and a drift extended from Broad Carr Road under a field called the Great Arm Royd. Armroyd Lane now intersects this field. In 1795 Elsecar's first proper shaft was opened in an area now known as Distillery Side, because a distillery opened there in 1814. It exported its numerous products, such as lamp black, tar and coloured varnishes, by canal. However, this was not successful and the distillery closed after only four years. The colliery was known as Elsecar New Colliery and was adjacent to the celebrated Newcomen-type beam engine.

Ironstone, which outcropped on Earl Fitzwilliam's land near Tankersley, was being dug for on John Shirt's farm at Hood Hill in 1793. In November 1795 John Darwin, a partner in the Sheffield firm Smith Stacey & Co., was operating the first furnace at Elsecar Ironworks, with coal supplied by the Fitzwilliam collieries and ironstone mined by Darwin's, for which the firm paid Lord Fitzwilliam the mineral rights. The ruins of this once substantial employer of labour in the district lie at the top of Forge Lane, behind what is today Elsecar Heritage Centre. By 1800 a second furnace was operating, and in the following decade the business flourished. Trade dropped dramatically in 1812 and a substantial number of workers were laid off. During December 1827 the firm of John Darwin & Company was declared bankrupt, which devastated families in Elsecar and Hoyland. The ironworks were then brought under the control of Earl Fitzwilliam.

Milton Ironworks was founded by the Masbrough firm Walker's and opened in 1802, the ironstone being mined on Fitzwilliam land at Tankersley. As at Elsecar Ironworks, a mile away, business at Walker's declined in the depression of 1812 but by the end of that year an upturn in fortune saw the firm making ready a new furnace, and by 1814 they were heavily involved in bridge building. Both Elsecar Ironworks and Walker's suffered a considerable drop in business at the end of the Napoleonic wars, and by 1822 Walker's had surrendered their lease to Lord Fitzwilliam. It was taken over by Henry Hartop, who secured a contract with the French government to build two suspension bridges. Some time later two brothers joined him in partnership, but after a falling out the partnership was dissolved and William and Thomas Graham carried on running Milton Ironworks as Graham & Co., while Henry Hartop became manager of Elsecar Ironworks for Lord Fitzwilliam. He lived at Hoyland Hall until 1841, when he moved to Barnbrough Hall. In 1844 he left Elsecar Ironworks.

At Milton Ironworks Graham's produced pig, rod, sheet and hoop iron, and manufactured steam engines, boilers and iron boats, in addition to bridge building. After a tragic accident in 1848 at one of the firm's ironstone pits in Tankersley Park, in which John Guest was killed at the age of 18, much to the surprise and dismay of the workforce, a twenty-one year lease was offered for anyone wishing to take on Milton Ironworks. The closure of the firm caused a great deal of anxiety.

In March 1849 Lord Fitzwilliam secured a contract with John Dawes, the joint owner with his brother of a large ironworks in the Midlands, to let both Milton and Elsecar Ironworks. The contract allowed for them to be run by his two sons, George and William Henry. The years that followed saw further expansion of the population of Elsecar and Hoyland. By the early 1880s George Dawes was running both ironworks without the assistance of his brother, who was living in Staffordshire. He hoped to find a buyer for both ironworks but prices had dropped considerably, and much to the dismay of Lord Fitzwilliam, on the expiry of the lease and the worker's contracts on 31 January 1884, both works closed. These closures caused panic and considerable hardship in the area. Many of the skilled workers moved to Parkgate Ironworks, near Rotherham, but it was the labourers who found great difficulty in finding work. There were empty houses in Elsecar and Hoyland, as people moved out of the district. Shopkeepers suffered severely and Elsecar Market closed down, never to re-open. The Market Hall served as a skating rink before being altered to provide a much-needed Public Hall, which was eventually renamed the Milton Hall in honour of the seventh Earl Fitzwilliam's son and heir, Viscount Milton. Although over eighty years have passed, many still refer to the Milton Hall as the Market Hall. As with several others in the district, old names die hard. The recreation ground known as the 'Forge' is a reminder of where Milton Ironworks once stood. In the 1960s one of the ponds which served the old ironworks, situated across the road from the Furnace Inn, was drained, and its site and that of the ironworks itself was used as a municipal rubbish tip.

Long after both the Milton and Elsecar forges had been closed, a small workforce was still employed by two iron-working concerns in Elsecar. Both were family-run businesses. The first, J. Davy and Co. Ltd, founded in 1869 by Jonathan Davy and run by four generations of the family until 23 May 1980, was a general ironfounder. On the day it closed its workforce consisted of Ryan Davy, his wife Mollie, and nine men. The premises they occupied were a former brewery owned by Richard Jukes. The fettling shop was once a public house connected to it. The distinctive lozenge-shaped Davy logo can still be seen on iron products such as manhole covers as far afield as Bradford and Kingston-upon-Hull. Lax's Foundry, which was situated next to J. Davy and Co. Ltd, traded until 1942, having been opened in 1876 by William Lax, a former partner of Jonathan Davy, and manufactured a variety of goods, including 'Yorkshire' kitchen ranges. The Cardigan Foundry Ltd carried on trading in Lax's old premises for some years afterwards.

During this period of industrial expansion in the mid-18th century and for a hundred years or so following, the village of Elsecar grew. Many of the houses built on the hillside rising from Church Street to the top of Stubbin, such as Darwins Yard, Evans Terrace, Wards Row, and Back Stubbin, were demolished in the two decades after the Second World War but there are some fine examples of workmen's cottages surviving. The

Fitzwilliam properties, mostly constructed in Elsecar Valley, are particularly attractive. The Old Row, consisting of fifteen cottages, was built in the 1790s. This was followed by the group of ten cottages now known as Station Row, which were designed by the eminent architect John Carr. He submitted plans for six different types of cottage for Elsecar colliers to Lord Fitzwilliam in 1795. He also designed four lodge-like properties near Skiers Hall, comprising two semi-detached houses between two detached houses, and some plans exist which are signed by Carr for other houses intended to be built in Elsecar. However, these were never constructed. The six cottages in Meadow Row situated next to the Ship Inn pre-date the adjacent twenty-eight cottages of Reform Row by at least forty-seven years. Reform Row was constructed during the latter part of the reign of William IV and first occupied in 1837, the year Victoria came to the throne. It was named after the 1832 Reform Act. Cobcar Terrace and Lime Kiln Terrace, commonly known as Rhubarb Row (so called because of the profusion of rhubarb once grown in the vicinity), at the end of the village and close to the Brampton Bierlow border, are of a later date, as are many of the houses in Fitzwilliam Street, most of which were built in the middle of the 19th century.

The Electra Palace opened in 1914 at the top of Stubbin, and is situated just before the Hoyland boundary. It had stalls seating only with double seats towards the rear, favoured by courting couples. It changed its name in the 1930s to the Futurist, a name which it kept until its closure as a cinema in 1986. It was refurbished and reverted to its original name, and operated as a pool hall and video games establishment for a brief period. The building is currently standing empty. *(George Hardy collection)*

Elsecar from Beacon fields, *c.* 1922. *(Walker's Newsagents collection)*

Holy Trinity Church, Elsecar, *c*. 1900. On Whit Monday 1841 the fifth Earl Fitzwilliam laid the foundation stone of Holy Trinity Church, Elsecar, which was built at his own expense at a cost of £2,500. Constructed in Early English style, with its main axis running from south to north, it took two years to build and opened for worship on Whit Monday 6 June 1843, having been consecrated by the Archbishop of York. For several years the church remained in the parish of All Saints, Wath-upon-Dearne, until the parish of Elsecar came into existence in 1855. *(George Hardy collection)*

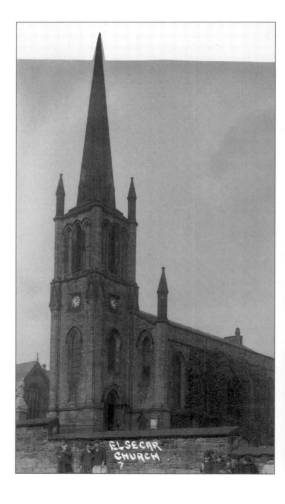

Originally, Holy Trinity Church had no vestry, but between 1870 and 1871 a combined organ chamber and vestry was built on the west side. On the night of Saturday 9 March 1905 the coke-fired boiler overheated, resulting in a fire that spread through a malfunctioning iron pipe and raged for one and a half hours, causing extensive damage to the chancel roof and choir stalls. The organ pipes suffered damage, not from the flames but from the gallons of water used to put out the fire. Worship continued in the nave during restoration, which cost £533 16*s* 2*d*. On Friday 9 June the church re-opened with a rebuilt organ and a new three-faced clocktower. The interior layout of the church has changed over the years, and there have been various bequests enabling improvements to take place. This photograph shows a group of children posing for the photographer, as he takes a snap of the south-east aspect of the church in the early 1920s. *(Walker's Newsagents collection)*

Howse's Corner from Forge Lane, *c. 1895*. The name has been used since about that time, after William and Martha Howse opened a confectionery, a grocery and general store. Howse's shop in the left foreground is at 1 Wentworth Road, situated opposite the Market Hotel at the junction of Fitzwilliam Street and Wentworth Road. Wath Road goes off to the right and Elsecar Market Hall, built by Earl Fitzwilliam and opened on Christmas Eve 1870, can be seen in the right-hand foreground, surrounded by a fence of stone posts and iron railings. The iron bollards placed on the street corners were to prevent carriage wheels mounting the pavement as the coachmen took the corners. There were originally four, one at each corner of the irregular crossroads. One remains today, protecting the corner of the New Yard, now Elsecar Heritage Centre. *(Ann Howse collection)*

Joseph Richard Howse was the eldest son of William and Martha. He was born in 1881, and after his marriage to Ellen Hesketh on 9 August 1902 lived at 8 Old Row. He had high hopes for a political career and began by serving as a Councillor for the Elsecar Ward, on Hoyland Nether UDC. He died in 1923 following a bout of influenza, before he could fulfil his political ambitions. Howse Street, Elsecar, was named in his memory. *(Ann Howse collection)*

The Howse family in the back yard of 1 Wentworth Road, 1911. Back row, left to right: Isadore, Jeremiah, William, John Thomas, Joseph Richard and Frank. Centre row: Mary, William Howse senior (1855–1926), Martha Howse (née Hirst, 1858–1919), Kate, Sarah Ann. Front row: Ivy and Martha. William and Martha's only other child, Edith Annie, died in infancy in 1898. William Howse was born in Netherton, Worcestershire. His father, Richard, was an oil and grease manufacturer, who later became a licensed victualler and proprietor of the Queen's Head, Kingswinford, which had its own brewery. William's mother, Sarah Ann (née Rowley), died at the age of 57 in April 1869 when William was 14. In February 1871 his father married a widow, Fanny Lewis; she was 39, he was 58. Sometime after his father's marriage to Fanny, William and his father fell out, possibly because William did not approve of the marriage. The situation became so strained that William could stand it no longer. He decided to make a new life for himself and moved away from the area in which he had grown up. He settled in Elsecar, where he was appointed foreman at Elsecar Ironworks by the Dawes brothers. William was known to the Dawes family through his father's industrial connections. Whether they brought him to Elsecar or whether he sought them out is not known, but the Dawes brothers certainly saw that he was given a position in which he could earn a reasonable living. William liked Elsecar and decided to settle there. He married when he was 25, in 1880. At the turn of the century he was well established in the area and financially secure. By this time all but one of William and Martha's twelve children had been born. He had expanded his business interests, and in addition to the shop he also dealt in insurance. As they grew older, William and Martha were able to take a back seat in the running of the shop, leaving the day-to-day management to two of their daughters. The younger daughter, Kate, was a popular local figure. She ran a mobile grocery and greengrocery business, visiting the surrounding villages by horse and cart. After the death of their parents Kate and Sarah Ann, who were unmarried, continued running Howse's shop until well into the 1960s. (Author's collection)

The first of the twin pit shafts of Earl Fitzwilliam's Simon Wood Colliery was being sunk when the Barnsley seam was reached at a depth of 93.5 yd on 1 September 1853. Known locally as the Planting Pit, it was also called the Bicycle Pit. The two pit shafts were only a few yards apart. The engine house had a headgear coming out of opposite sides, with a single pulley attached. The two winding ropes were attached to the same drum, which caused the pulleys to revolve in the same direction as each other, hence the nickname the Bicycle Pit. This colliery ceased production on 29 May 1903. The EFW Flour Mill, built by Earl Fitzwilliam in 1842 is in the left background. Behind the colliery chimney can be seen Reform Row. *(George Hardy collection)*

Elsecar Canal Basin, *c.* 1885. The building on the extreme left of the photograph is the EFW Flour Mill. The tall chimney dominating the centre left skyline belongs to Simon Wood Colliery. Judging by how busy it is in this photograph, it seems hardly surprising that Elsecar was referred to as the port of Elsecar on some official records. After the closure of Hemingfield Colliery in May 1920 barges no longer travelled to Elsecar and the canal gradually deteriorated. Locks were dismantled and nature began to take over where man left off. However, in the 1970s the Cortonwood Project drew up plans for the rejuvenation of the Elsecar branch of the Dearne and Dove Canal, and that was the first step towards putting the canal back into use. *(Edward Ellis collection)*

The sinking of Elsecar Main Colliery, *c.* 1905. This view was taken looking toward Royds Cottages in Royds Lane. *(George Hardy collection)*

As early as 1903 there were rumours that Earl Fitzwilliam intended to sink a new colliery near the site of Simon Wood Colliery. On 17 July 1905 the sinking of what was to be known as Elsecar Main Colliery began. Sinking of the No. 2 shaft began on 19 April 1906 and production began in February 1908. Coal was reached at the Parkgate seam at a depth of 350 yd on 18 February. A total of 457,706 bricks were used in the construction of the colliery chimney. The total height of the chimney was 192 ft but seen from ground level it reached a height of 184 ft, the chimney being completed on 28 October 1908 at a cost of £1,291 17s 11½d. Coal was later taken from the Silkstone, Thorncliffe and Haigh Moor seams. This photograph shows the colliery in the mid-1920s. Local people still referred to it as the 'new pit' right up to its closure seventy-eight years later, at which time 730 men were working there. During its peak production period in the 1960s Elsecar Main was producing one million tons of coal per year. *(Walker's Newsagents collection)*

Church Street, 1890s. On the right, the tall roof of the first large gable is the grocery store belonging to the Church Street branch of the Barnsley British Co-operative Society. The second gable belongs to the Wesleyan Reform chapel, built in 1859. The new brick-built boys' section of Elsecar Church of England School, built to accommodate Elsecar's increasing population, masks the older mixed school, which was built in dressed sandstone in 1852, thanks to the benevolence of the sixth Earl Fitzwilliam; it was a larger replacement for a school built by the fourth Earl Fitzwilliam in 1836 on Distillery Side. Holy Trinity Church can be seen beyond. It is interesting to see the long tract of empty land between the houses on the left and the school. (*Chris Thawley collection*)

Hill Street (formerly Cobcar) from Fitzwilliam Street, *c.* 1900. Church Street can be seen on the right. (*Margaret Gaddass collection*)

Isadore Howse, on the left, and Herbert Thickett, landlord of the Market Hotel, outside the dovecote in the garden of Elsecar's largest public house, *c.* 1902. After his premature death in 1923, the licence was taken over by Herbert's wife, Clara B. Thickett. The Thicketts continued running the Market Hotel for another generation, when Herbert and Clara's son Horace took over and ran it with his wife Gladys, before they retired to Wentworth in the early 1970s. The Market, as it is known today, has been sensitively enlarged without altering the basic elements that have made this fine public house so successful. It has retained the four bars (separate rooms with their own distinctive identity, all served from one central area), and an unusual lobby where many locals gather. A pool room has been tastefully converted from the old vehicular entry and includes its own bar, and also a well-appointed function room, also with its own bar, situated on the first floor, are relatively new additions. *(Ann Howse collection)*

The Old Horse, 1906. The Old Horse was a great local tradition which raised money for good causes locally up until the Second World War. This group of local mummers toured pubs at Christmas time and was occasionally invited to Wentworth Woodhouse to perform for the Earl and Countess Fitzwilliam and their guests. In addition to the Old Horse there were other characters, who were each introduced by an accordion player who sang the appropriate doggerel verse for each character. The opening of Elsecar Heritage Centre saw a revival of the Old Horse, much to the delight of many local residents who had fond memories of it. The only person I have been able to identify is Tabba Evans, who is kneeling on the front row, wearing a striped hat. *(Jack Howse collection)*

Reform Row decorated for the visit of their Majesties King George V and Queen Mary to Elsecar Colliery, 9 July 1912. The late Cllr Dennis Eaden remembered the visit and recalled: 'My first recollection is the visit of King George to Elsecar Main in 1912. I was given a flag and put behind a roped fence opposite the Ship Inn.' *(Jack Howse collection)*

The arrival of the King's car at Elsecar Main Colliery. *(Chris Thawley collection)*

The visit of their Majesties King George V and Queen Mary to Elsecar, 9 July 1912. Emerging from the doorway on the left are Maud, Countess Fitzwilliam and Her Majesty Queen Mary. His Majesty the King is in the right foreground with William Charles de Meuron, seventh Earl Fitzwilliam, to his Majesty's right. *(George Hardy collection)*

The Crown Inn, before the First World War. As well as being landlord of this popular Elsecar public house, Samuel D. Smith also had a transport company. He owned several motor vehicles which he hired out for weddings and other events. The vehicles were often displayed on the large forecourt in front of the Crown Inn. Mr Smith was landlord until 1941. *(Margaret Gaddass collection)*

Elsecar station, *c.* 1910. Variously known as Elsecar station and Elsecar and Hoyland station, it was opened by the Midland Railway Company on 1 July 1897. They built shelters on each platform with a first-class and a general waiting room. There was a goods yard to the right with its own sidings. The large water tank can be seen on the left and nearer the bridge is a water crane. The gable of the booking office can be seen on the right. Elsecar was a very well-kept station and won many competitions over the years. Flowers were planted on the two bankings and the platforms were kept in good order. Since the withdrawal of station staff in the 1960s, Elsecar station has been kept in a reasonable order. The old waiting rooms were partially demolished to provide open shelters. *(Frank Kelly collection)*

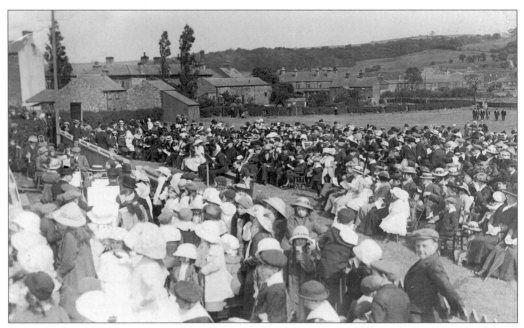

The Hospital Sing gathering on Elsecar cricket field, *c.* 1909. This event was traditionally held on Elsecar Feast Sunday, which was always the week after Whitsuntide. The boy leaning on the picket fence in the foreground looking directly at the camera is Ron Taylor. *(Doreen Howse collection)*

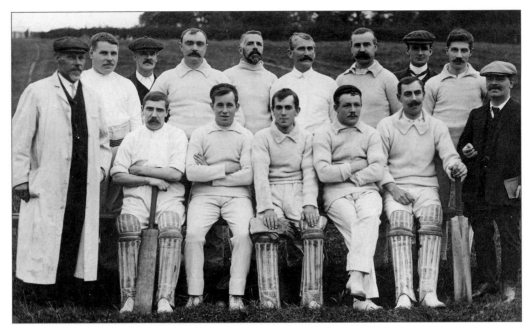

Elsecar Thursday Cricket Club, *c.* 1912. The third man from the left in the back row is Sam Wood; the fourth man standing next to him is Herbert Thickett. Jim March, who was a postman, is standing on the right of the front row, wearing a flat cap. *(Jack Howse collection)*

In the orchard of the Market Hotel, *c.* 1918. On the left Mr Lusby, who lived in the Old Row and was the Thicketts' gardener, leans on his fork; his assistant stands next to him. Alan Thickett stands next to his father Herbert, and Horace Thickett standing on the right completes the picture. *(Jack Howse collection)*

Elsecar cricket field, early 1920s. Seated on the bench are Mr Butterworth on the left, Mr Beech, third from the left, and Sam Evans on the extreme right. *(Jack Howse collection)*

Fitzwilliam Street looking towards Howse's Corner, *c.* 1925. The New Yard can be seen facing the end of the street. On the left is the Miners' Lodging House built by the fifth Earl Fitzwilliam in 1850 to accommodate young, single miners but it was not a successful idea, the miners preferring to live elsewhere. For a short time it was used as a social club and was jocularly known as the Bun and Milk Club as it didn't serve alcohol. That closed in 1854. A boys' club, subsidised by Lord Fitzwilliam and known as the Low Club, occupied it from 1865. From 1902 the village 'bobby' lived in part of it, at the opposite end of the building to the steward of the boys' club. The middle section became a club for the colliery workshops, but after the Fitzwilliam mining enterprises were nationalised in 1947 much of the building stood empty. Messrs J. Priestman and Co. Ltd, a burling and weaving company, took over for a few years before Swift's, a local joinery business, traded from there until 1973. The building became severely dilapidated and there was a threat of demolition. Fortunately a joint effort by North Cheshire Housing Association and Barnsley MBC resulted in conversion into fourteen flats, at a cost of £260,000. £40,000 came in a grant from the Department of the Environment; the remainder was loaned by Barnsley MBC. The newly named Fitzwilliam Lodge was officially opened by the Mayor of Barnsley, Cllr John Wake, in 1982. It is Listed Grade II. Locals still refer to the building as the Bun and Milk Club. *(Margaret Gaddass collection)*

George Barker Lee Summerscales lived at 68 Wath Road in the well-proportioned terrace that was in reality Lime Kiln Terrace but more commonly known as Rhubarb Row. He came to Elsecar to work at Elsecar Main Colliery at the age of 15, having been brought up at Thorne Hill, Dewsbury. He was always a very dapper dresser and noted for wearing spats. His brother Hilton died at the age of 41, as a result of injuries he received in 1934 in an accident at Elsecar Main, when a cage he was travelling in, overshot the landing stage on returning to the surface, crashing into the winding gear. Many serious injuries were sustained. George Summerscales died in 1982 at the age of 85; his wife of 64 years, Ethel, died the following year aged 87. They had two children, Doreen and Gerald, who became a pit overman at Elsecar main. *(Jack Howse collection)*

The Skiers family takes its name from the hamlet within Hoyland's boundaries. During the 14th century members of that family were also living at Alderthwaite, which was a hamlet at one time but today is the large farm lying close to the top of Burying Lane. The Skiers Hall Estate remained in the Skiers family during the medieval period and various members appear on documents connected with land throughout the area. The estate changed hands several times until it was purchased by the second Earl of Strafford, who on his death bequeathed it to Robert Monckton. The first Marquess of Rockingham purchased the estate shortly before his death in 1750, and it has remained in the ownership of his heirs ever since. This 1920s view shows the 14th-century Skiers Hall after it had been converted into cottages. Skiers Hall Farm was situated adjacent to the hall. It is now the largest property in the hamlet, as the 14th-century hall itself was demolished in 1951. *(Walker's Newsagents collection)*

A group of volunteers assembled on the steps of Milton Hall during the General Strike of 1926, when the hall was being used as a soup kitchen. In the front row, left to right, are Fred Streams and Isadore Howse. Also among the group are Mr Widdowson, Mr Butterworth, Mr Walker, Albert Evans, John Eden, Melvin Hague, Harry Donald, another Mr Walker, Albert Wilkinson, Alf Oldknow, Herman Carter, John Speight, Jonathan Eden, Mrs Stenton, Mrs Howse and Miss Sarah Howse. *(Jack Howse collection)*

Thomas Walker (1867–1948), father of Elsecar's popular midwife, Nurse Nora Walker (1899–1989), of Skiers Hall, Elsecar. Tom Walker started working at Hemingfield Colliery at the age of 14, but in 1918 he had to give up mining as he suffered with persistent rheumatism. He spent his time carving coal with an ordinary kitchen knife strengthened with a brass handle. The memorial to King George V was presented to Elsecar Midland Working Men's Club: the inscription on the base was ornamented in gilt. His sought-after carvings included a wide range of subjects, ranging from prayer books (Lady Joan and Lady Donatia Fitzwilliam were pleased to accept prayer books, suitably inscribed, on the occasion of their weddings) to clogs. Many of his larger carvings were memorials of some kind. *(Margaret Gaddass collection)*

Beattie's Big Trip, 1936. Mr Beattie of Beattie's Busy Corner, Hoyland, was a great organiser, helping to arrange festive and commemorative occasions, and the event for which he was best known was the annual Big Trip to Blackpool Illuminations each autumn, leaving on a weekday morning and returning the next day in the small hours. To ensure everything went off successfully Mr Beattie was in attendance. Older people still talk about the trips, which for some were the highlight of the year. *(Martha Nelder collection)*

Elsecar Band outside their headquarters, the Market Hotel, 1938. In the centre of the front row holding his baton is the conductor Edwin 'Teddy' Williamson. Front row, left to right: H. Hague, F. Dakin, H. Glover, F. Beech, P. Lewis (sitting on floor), G. Maca, J. Chricton, Bill Carr, A.R. Easthorpe. Middle row: E. Rutter, J. Beaumont, Jack Swallow, H. Naylor, H. Beaumont, T. Townsend, J. Bedford, F. Williamson. Back row: Mr Wildman, A. Evans, C. Hill, Walt Whitehouse. Others in the group include Oscar Airey, B. Carey, Walt Quinny, L. Loy, Mr Hill and Mr Tasker. *(Doreen Howse collection)*

Hilda and Harry Ackroyd of 13 Ebenezer Place during a VE Day party held in the square between Ebenezer Place and Church Street. (*Martha Nelder collection*)

Elsecar has some of the most beautiful countryside in Yorkshire on its doorstep and there are many walks which take in some of the most spectacular views of the surrounding area. Here a group has walked from Elsecar through Low Wood, and rests for a few moments by the stile at the Wentworth side of the wood. Left to right: Jack Stewart, his father-in-law George Littlewood, seated on the stile is George Nelder, behind him sitting on the fence is his son Terence (Terry) Nelder, the Stewart twins Joan and John, and John Prescott, who was the School Attendance Officer, or as he tended to be known the 'School Bobby'. (*Martha Nelder collection*)

Elsecar Church of England School Sports Day, 1951. In the photograph is Mary Whitehouse, who is standing in the back row holding her daughter Margaret (now Mrs Les Gaddass). Also in the photograph, standing at the rear on the right-hand side in front of the girl by the fence, is Eve Wood. *(Margaret Gaddass collection)*

A float gets ready for the Coronation celebrations in the playground of Elsecar Church of England School, 1953. Harry Ackroyd dressed as queen has a crown placed on his head by Les Stenton. A Church Street resident holds the cushion and the two attendants are Doreen Turner (left) and Julie Bamforth. *(Martha Nelder collection)*

CHAPTER THREE

ELSECAR-BY-THE-SEA

Elsecar reservoir was created by damming Harley Dike to feed the Dearne and Dove Canal at Elsecar Basin. The construction of the canal was authorised by Act of Parliament in 1793; work began in January 1795. Until well into the 20th century the reservoir was a larger expanse of water than it is today; it stretched under the bridge to the Wentworth side of Watery Lane and under the bridge in Burying Lane. The water level was allowed to drop between the two world wars, when there was concern that the dam wall had been damaged by subsidence. It is still a lovely stretch of water and popular with anglers, as well as being home to several species of waterfowl. The dam wall lasted until the early 1990s, when it was partly replaced by a reinforced, sloping concrete structure.

In about 1910 a Sheffield barber called Herbert Parkin opened a shop in Stubbin. He was an accomplished amateur photographer and spent his spare time recording local subjects. He took some views of Elsecar reservoir and the surrounding area and sent them to the *Sheffield Star*, which published them with the caption 'Elsecar-by-the-Sea'. Mr Parkin's photographs struck the right note with the population of Sheffield and, as Elsecar could easily be reached by rail, there began an exodus to the village to escape the grime of the city, a special treat for children who rarely saw the countryside. The sobriquet Elsecar-by-the-Sea lasted for decades. The late Dennis Eaden remembered being stopped at about 5.15 one morning by some foreign tourists, as recently as the mid-1970s, who asked him if they were on the right road for Elsecar-by-the-Sea.

Elsecar proved so popular an attraction that it was decided to capitalise on this, and the idea of creating a public park was born. It began with Hoyland UDC building a refreshment room. A large artificial beach was created and boats sailed on the reservoir, pronounced by many locally 'reservoy', but referred to by many during that period as the lake, and by others as Elsecar Lido. The park was divided into two main areas, known as the top and bottom park. The top park is adjacent to the reservoir, where the various joy rides can be found and where galas and fun fairs have been held; the bottom park is principally devoted to flower beds, and contains the bandstand and children's corner.

There are fewer facilities today than there used to be. However, the refreshment room is still there and has recently been refurbished. Elsecar Park has some flower beds, an attractive bandstand and a dike which can be crossed by way of two bridges. The dike winds its way from the new dam wall, through the bottom park and under a little bridge, crossing beneath Wentworth Road, where it emerges alongside a large car park, at the end of which it disappears underground. The park also boasts a pitch and putt golf course, which has been a popular attraction since the 1950s.

There have been two paddling pools since the park opened. The most recent was constructed in the 1950s close to the site of the original which it replaced. Its loss is a great shame, as much pleasure was derived from it on hot summer days. Although Hoyland itself boasts a sports centre with two swimming pools, they offer little compensation for the toddlers and young visitors.

The tiered gardens with their recessed seats and numerous flower beds are kept in reasonable order, but they are pitifully mundane compared with their appearance in years gone by: the entire area has suffered greatly since the demise of Hoyland UDC.

An early view of Elsecar Park, from the top park, looking towards the Wentworth Road entrance, c. 1920. Note the 'keep off the grass' sign. The fields to the left of the path are where the pitch and putt golf course was laid out three decades later. *(Walker's Newsagents collection)*

The lower section of the tiered gardens in the bottom park, 1920s. *(Walker's Newsagents collection)*

A view from the bottom park towards the bailiff's house, known as Pond House, in the top park, *c.* 1920. This photograph was taken from where the bandstand is presently situated. Note the original position of the bandstand, adjacent to the refreshment room on the extreme right skyline. Pond House was demolished in the 1980s. *(Walker's Newsagents collection)*

The upper part of the bottom park, showing the avenue of trees which now provides a pleasant shaded walkway. In the previous view only saplings were growing by the hedge running alongside Pond House. *(Author's commission)*

The dike which runs through the bottom park. This view shows one of the two bridges, with its original wooden balustrade. The area to the right has traditionally been one of the most peaceful places within the park – a location where one could sit and enjoy quiet contemplation. *(Walker's Newsagents collection)*

A view of the same bridge from the opposite direction, 1930s. Note the impressive balustrade. *(George Hardy collection)*

The most recent metal balustrades which adorn the present-day bridges, 1999. This view shows a marked contrast to the park seen on the previous page. Compare the area to the left of the bridge with the same area as it appears today. *(Author's commission)*

A view across the dike to where there were once manicured lawns and well-tended flower beds, July 1999. *(Author's commission)*

The original paddling pool, situated in a clearing beneath the dam wall in the bottom park. The photograph was taken *c.* 1931. The little girl on the left whose image is slightly blurred, is Kathleen Scholfield (now Mrs Hirst). She is being held by her sister Peggy Schofield (now Mrs Grantham). The girl in the right foreground, wearing a white angora hat is Grace Hirst. (*Walker's Newsagents Collection*)

Elsecar reservoir, *c.* 1920. This photograph, taken by Roy Colville and published as a postcard by I.L. Walker with the caption 'The Lake Elsecar', clearly illustrates the beauty of the surrounding countryside, which made Elsecar such a popular location for a day out for city dwellers. (*Walker's Newsagents collection*)

Such was the popularity of Elsecar-by-the-Sea that a full range of postcards was produced to show the various attractions the resort had to offer. This one, entitled 'The Landing Stage, Elsecar Harbour', shows one of the many rowing boats which were available for hire. The dam wall can be seen behind the man standing on the portable jetty. (*Margaret Gaddass collection*)

The landing stage from the opposite direction, showing the beach and the many visitors who have congregated in the top park. The hamlet surrounding Skiers Hall itself can be seen in the distance. (*Walker's Newsagents collection*)

Another early postcard showing 'The Beach, Elsecar-by-the-Sea'. *(George Hardy collection)*

A very full reservoir with scores of people enjoying the delights of the water and Elsecar sands. *(George Hardy collection)*

'The Beach, Elsecar', 1920s. *(Walker's Newsagents collection)*

The same location as the previous photograph, July 1999. The beach is no more, as it has long since been overgrown. Elsecar Reservoir and surrounding land were designated a local nature reserve by Barnsley Metropolitan Borough Council in May 1996. In my own opinion it is a good thing that the reservoir is attracting different kinds of wildlife and some rare species including great crested grebes and lesser spotted woodpeckers, but surely it is still a sufficiently large expanse of water, with plenty of cover on the Watery Lane and Burying Lane fringes to provide habitats for birds, waterfowl and animals, without the nature reserve having to encroach into the relatively short stretch of bank that can be reached from the top park. *(Author's commission)*

Two local youngsters Terence (Terry) Nelder (left) and John Stewart enjoy a game of pooh sticks in Elsecar Park, 1946. *(Martha Nelder collection)*

A view from the edge of the top park across the eighteen-hole pitch and putt golf course, towards the village, 1999. *(Author's commission)*

The bottom park, 1950s. *(George Hardy collection)*

A similar view, 1999. The arrival of the present park keeper has seen a marked improvement in the maintenance and general appearance of the flower beds. With limited funds placed at his disposal it must be a constant uphill struggle. He also provides a hearty welcome to visitors to the refreshment room. It is a great shame that there is no longer a large enough staff working in the park to support him. *(Author's commission)*

Yet another postcard view of the attractions that Elsecar-by-the-Sea had to offer, 'The Promenade, Elsecar', early 1920s. In reality this is Watery Lane. *(Walker's Newsagents collection)*

The Promenade, Elsecar, in winter. *(Walker's Newsagents collection)*

Lake Elsecar in winter, 1920s. *(Walker's Newsagents collection)*

A postcard view of Harley Dike running into the reservoir, one of the many views available at that time. This one is entitled 'Winter's Sway'. *(Walker's Newsagents collection)*

A composite postcard of the attractions to be found at Elsecar, photographed by Roy Colville and published by Lichie Walker, 1920s. (*Walker's Newsagents collection*)

An amusing postcard published by Lichie Walker and photographed by Roy Colville. (*Walker's Newsagents collection*)

WENTWORTH

This chapter covers Wentworth, Wentworth Woodhouse and the Fitzwilliam Wentworth Estate. Four Saxon lords had shares in the 'Winterworth' estate, Wentworth's name in the Domesday Survey. The name Wentworth has two interpretations: the first is a pleasant abode, 'went' signifying fair or white and 'worth' a dwelling place; the other is a high but cultivated spot, where the cold was severe but the land productive. It is also possible that the name Winterworth signifies a winter residence of some importance. Before the Norman Conquest Roger de Busli of Hallamshire owned a portion of the estate, but after 1066 the bulk of it passed to the Lords of Skipton, who sub-let the land to the Flemings from Wath-upon-Dearne, before it fell into the ownership of the Canons of Bolton Abbey. During the reign of Henry III (1216–72) William de Wyntword, whose name later evolved into Wentworth, acquired a substantial portion of the estate by marriage to Emma, daughter of William Wodehouse of 'Woodhous', that name referring possibly to a timber house which existed on the site. Whether the joining of these two families in marriage resulted in the naming of the family seat Wentworth Woodhouse cannot be accurately determined.

After the dissolution of the monasteries by Henry VIII the remaining lands previously owned by the Canons of Bolton became part of the Wentworth estate. The original Wentworth Woodhouse was most likely a timber structure which was enlarged, altered, modified and perhaps even completely rebuilt several times, until it eventually evolved into the house built in the classical manner as shown in an engraving in 1630, a style first introduced by Inigo Jones after he returned from Italy in 1615. From the thirteenth century onwards the Wentworth family were prominent in the affairs of the West Riding. Their estate grew in size and until 1656, when the Second Earl of Strafford sold it for £28,000, the Wentworths owned another Yorkshire estate, brought into the family by the first Earl's grandmother, Margaret Gascoigne. Gawthorpe Hall stood on the opposite bank of the lake where Harewood House was later built. From the time of the great Earl of Strafford's grandfather in the early sixteenth century more is known about the family who resided at Wentworth Woodhouse. The village of Wentworth and its satellite hamlets evolved to suit the changing requirements of the great house and estate, which its inhabitants served.

Although they had been an important Yorkshire family for over 300 years, the Wentworths came into greater prominence in the 17th century. Thomas Wentworth was born on 13 April 1593, at the house of his maternal grandfather Sir Robert Atkinson, in Chancery Lane, London. Much has been written about a man considered by many eminent historians to have been one of the greatest English statesmen ever to have lived.

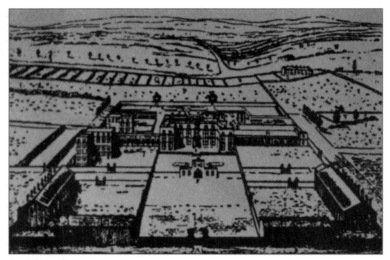

After attending St John's College, Cambridge, Thomas Wentworth entered the Inner Temple as a student in 1607. In October 1611 he married Lady Margaret Clifford, daughter of the Earl of Cumberland, and that December was knighted by James I. He sat in the so called 'Addled Parliament' of 1614 and that year became the Second Baronet and head of the family, on the death of his father Sir William. His first marriage was childless, and Lady Margaret died in 1622. Wentworth sat for Pontefract in the parliament of 1624 and the following year married Lady Arabella Holles, daughter of the Earl of Clare. In the first parliament of Charles I in 1625 Sir Thomas Wentworth sat for Yorkshire. He had already carved himself an influential career in politics, occupying senior positions in the north of England. At first he was opposed to the King, but after the assassination of the King's favourite the Duke of Buckingham, Charles won him over. Wentworth's considerable abilities earned him honours and even higher office. In 1629 he was created Baron Wentworth, and later that same year Viscount Wentworth; this was followed by his appointment as President of the Council of the North on 25 December. His much-loved wife Arabella, an accomplished linguist and great beauty, died in October 1631.

In January 1632 he was appointed Lord Deputy of Ireland and in October that same year married Margaret Rhodes, daughter of Sir Godfrey Rhodes of Great Houghton. He went to Dublin in June 1633. Wentworth's time in Ireland and the policy he implemented there, known as 'Thorough', is legendary, as are his dealings with the problems brewing in Scotland, where his friend and ally Archbishop Laud exercised similar powers to his own. They were both by temperament authoritarian men of action. The policy of 'Thorough', which they implemented ruthlessly, was a course which was hard to stomach for the King and even the most supportive of his subjects. The policy emphasised the Crown's power and individual responsibility among the King's servants, combined with a hard-hearted inquiry into abuses and a merciless crushing of opponents. Given full powers, and on virtually every occasion the full support of Whitehall, Wentworth ruled Ireland like a king. In six years he reorganised the finances, the army, navy and law courts. He also brought new blood into the Protestant Church, increased revenue from the customs, began industrial projects and checked piracy. The two great changes which he was responsible for regarded his financial policy, which was so effective that no subsidy was required from England, and he pursued the Laudian policy among the Irish Protestants of enforcing discipline upon the clergy and taking back ecclesiastical land from the laity. His success in these areas aroused discontent among the influential classes in Ireland, and the threat to landed and mercantile property was a cause of considerable unease, creating a host of enemies throughout the land. This print shows Wentworth Woodhouse in 1630. *(Author's collection with permission of the Fitzwilliam Wentworth Estate)*

In 1638–9 the whole fabric of Charles I's government was threatened by the Scottish revolt against Laud's ecclesiastical policy. The King turned to Wentworth for help. In September 1639 Wentworth returned to England as requested, for His Majesty required closer counsel, having ruled for eleven years without summoning Parliament. In January 1640 Wentworth was created Lord Lieutenant of Ireland, Baron Raby and Earl of Strafford, Newmarch and Oversley. Strafford or Strafforth is the name of the wapentake (division of the shire) in which Wentworth Woodhouse is situated. It is as Thomas Wentworth, Earl of Strafford or the great Earl of Strafford, that history remembers him. He returned to Dublin on 18 March 1640, charged with the task of raising money for the

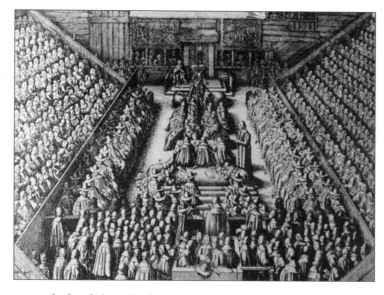

pending war with Scotland. As soon as the session had ended Strafford returned to Westminster to take his seat in the House of Lords in the 'Short Parliament', which he had advised the King to call. When Parliament refused to grant the King's requests until their grievances had been addressed, he dissolved it.

Strafford had made many enemies at court, as exceptionally intelligent and gifted men often have. Petty jealousy and envy compounded previously minor transgressions into hatred, and many former friends in the Commons, influenced heavily by their Puritan members, saw Strafford as a major stumbling block in their disputes with the King's authority. Unable to pursue his policy in Scotland without sufficient funds, the King summoned Parliament. The 'Long Parliament' met on 3 November 1640. His Majesty needed Strafford's counsel and sent for him. Strafford left Wentworth Woodhouse for London on 6 November with, in his own words, 'more dangers beset, I believe, than ever a man went out of Yorkshire'. After his arrival in London on 9 November his enemies, who included John Pym and his own brother-in-law, Denzil Holles, wasted no time. They wanted to remove Strafford from the equation and weaken the King's authority. Strafford was the most gifted statesman in the land; the King relied on his judgement and trusted him. With Strafford at his side, Charles I had a greater chance of achieving his aims and stamping his authority on those who were rallying against him. Without Strafford at his side, the King would be easier to deal with. Strafford's enemies impeached him on nine general and twenty-eight specific allegations, and he was committed to the Tower of London on 25 November.

On 21 January 1641 the detailed charges were brought before the House of Commons. After protracted legal wrangling Strafford's trial commenced in Westminster Hall on 22 March. He defended himself with great skill. There was nothing treasonable in what Strafford had been accused of, although it was on a charge of High Treason that his enemies wished to see him brought down. He stood his ground, and by 10 April it was clear that a guilty verdict could not be brought. He could be found guilty by Act of Parliament, a path seldom used to bring down a minister of the Crown. Known as a Bill of Attainder, it was a short cut to enable Strafford's enemies to find him guilty. In simple terms, the Attainder was a tool enabling those who wished to charge an individual with certain crimes to find him automatically guilty, providing the Attainder was endorsed by the King himself. Pym was apprehensive about how the Lords would receive the Attainder but in the Commons he had prepared his ground well. It was introduced, and began its passage through the parliamentary system.

On 13 April, his 48th birthday, Strafford came to Westminster Hall to defend himself for the last time. He addressed himself exclusively to the Lords, giving a powerful speech: many of those who witnessed it were moved to tears. More than half of those assembled were in his favour. Pym remained steadfast in his resolve to destroy Strafford. The Commons debated their bill against Strafford. It had a rough passage and its eventual presentation to the King was only achieved after threats and accusations had been exercised against members of both houses. It seems inconceivable that such was their hatred, Pym and his supporters proceeded on the premise that Strafford was guilty, even if legally he was innocent. This copy of an engraving by Wenceslas Hollar shows the trial of Strafford in Westminster Hall. Lord Strafford is shown in the centre foreground. The boxes seen at the rear were specially constructed to accommodate the King and Royal family during the trial; today a brass plaque marks the spot where Strafford sat in Westminster Hall. *(Author's collection)*

A. Doctor Vſher, Lord
te of Ireland,
B. the Sherifes of London
C. the Earle of Straffor
D. his kindred and Frie

The Commons passed the bill on 21 April by a majority of 204 to 59. In breach of parliamentary privilege, the names of the 59 members who had voted against the bill were posted up throughout London, with the caption 'These are the Straffordians, betrayers of their country.' Two thousand citizens of London invaded Parliament with a petition asking for Strafford's life. On 23 April the King sent a secret message to Strafford assuring him that he: 'shall not suffer in life, honour or fortune'. The bill received its first reading in the Lords on 26 April. Riots, threats, abuse and general social unrest were the order of the day, as Pym and his cronies strived to bring about Strafford's end. Timidity prevailed in the Lords. The whole bench of bishops took it upon themselves to decide that they were disqualified from voting. On 8 May the bill was finally put to the vote. Only 48 peers of the 147 entitled to vote took their seats. The Bill of Attainder was passed by thirty-seven votes to eleven. Now only the King stood in its way. His Majesty refused to sign. Before, during and in the wake of Strafford's trial his enemies had been stirring up trouble. They encouraged the mob to refer to Strafford as 'Black Tom Wentworth', assuring them that all would be well in the land if Strafford was got rid of. The message of the mob was that Black Tom Wentworth must die. Still the King refused to betray his most loyal subject, ally and friend. But on 9 May the mob stormed Whitehall Palace and threats were made against the lives of the Queen and the Queen Mother. The Constable of the Tower, Lord Newport, declared that he would have his prisoner killed if the King refused to sign Strafford's Attainder. Perhaps in fear for the safety of his family, or because of the hopelessness of the situation, the King gave Strafford's Attainder the Royal Assent and the Bill became an Act of Attainder. As the King laid down the pen, tears gathered in his eyes and he said 'My Lord of Strafford's condition is happier than mine.' With this signature, many believe, Charles I sealed not just his subject's fate but his own as well. On hearing the news late in the evening on 9 May, Strafford replied to Dudley Carlton, its bearer: 'Put not your trust in princes nor in the sons of men for in them there is no salvation.' Strafford's honours were forfeited and he was now simply Thomas Wentworth again. His enemies had got what they wanted, but perhaps even they had some scruples, for no one spoke of enforcing the law to its full limit, as the Act of Attainder provided that he should be hanged, drawn and quartered, as a traitor. His enemies were content to see him beheaded. The execution was a great event, and over 200,000 people watched it, a number which at that time accounted for the greater part of the population of London. Special stands were hurriedly built. In the famous engraving by Wenceslas Holler seen here, the scene is clearly depicted.

On 12 May 1641 at 2 o'clock in the morning the crowds were already gathering on Tower Hill. At 11 o'clock Sir William Balfour came to see if the prisoner was ready. Dressed in black, as was his custom, he was calmly waiting with his two chaplains. Balfour was afraid that the mob would tear Wentworth to pieces, advising him to send for his coach. Wentworth declined, saying: 'No, I would sooner look death in the face and I hope the people too; I care not how I die whether by the hand of the executioner or by the madness and fury of the people; if that may give them better content it is all one to me.' As the prisoner with the accompanying party of officials and friends walked to Tower Hill, they passed the window of Wentworth's fellow prisoner Archbishop Laud, who was shortly to suffer a similar fate. Wentworth knelt down and said 'Your prayers and your blessing.' Laud held out his hand, was grief-stricken and fainted. As Wentworth continued on his journey he called out 'Farewell, my lord; God protect your innocency.' As the party made their way through the gates, a narrow pathway cleared. Wentworth was saluted by some and he walked with dignity, hat in hand, acknowledging the courtesies extended to him. Some commented afterwards that he walked like a great general, marching to victory. On the scaffold he made several speeches. He spoke to the crowd asking them, when the times changed, to judge him by his actions. His companions had joined him on the scaffold, with officials, clergy and those there expressly to record what was said or done for posterity. He took each one by the hand. Taking off his doublet and putting on a white cap, he called 'Where is the man that shall do this last office?' The executioner, Richard Brandon, stepped forward to ask his forgiveness; Wentworth replied: 'I forgive you and all the world.' After refusing a blindfold with the words 'Nay, for I will see it done,' he knelt in prayer for a few moments with the Bishop of Armagh on one side, the minister on the other. After first trying out the block, he laid his head down and the executioner severed it from his body with one blow. The dripping head was held up by Brandon to the words 'God save the King'. Horsemen rode out from all four corners of the scaffold to be first to spread the news, calling out 'His head is off! His head is off!' The body was not buried in St Peter ad Vincula, within the precincts of the Tower, nor was his head put on a pike and displayed on London Bridge. During the afternoon following his execution Wentworth's head and body mysteriously disappeared; they were spirited away to Yorkshire for a decent burial. Perhaps a blind eye was turned to the removal of the body from the Tower of London. Everyone concerned with the affair was aware that Wentworth was killed for convenience and not for any crime. A memorial erected by his son William is in the lady chapel in the old church at Wentworth. On the scaffold at his own execution in January 1649, Charles I made reference to Strafford in his speech to the crowd: 'An unjust sentence that I suffered to take effect, is punished now by an unjust sentence on me.' Of Strafford, the distinguished author of *England under the Stuarts*, George Macaulay Trevelyan OM, wrote: 'He served England well, for he dignified her history. He showed that the cause of tyranny did not fail among us, first of all great nations, because among us it lacked princely intellect or royal valour.' *(Author's collection)*

Strafford's honours were forfeited by his Attainder but were restored to his son William, then aged 14, by the King in December 1641. He was created first Earl of Strafford of the second creation, but this was altered when his father's Attainder was reversed by Parliament in 1662, when he became second Earl of Strafford of the first creation. He married twice but died without issue in 1695. The Strafford title became extinct. His heir was a son of his sister Anne, who had married Edward, second Baron Rockingham. The nephew, Thomas Watson, was his parents' third and second surviving son. He changed his name to Watson Wentworth and was known as 'His Honour Wentworth'. The letters patent of the title Baron Raby allowed for that title to be passed to a 23-year-old great-nephew of the first Earl of Strafford, another Thomas Wentworth (1672–1739). He effectively became head of the Wentworths, with a title but none of their estates. The story of the rivalry which resulted between the two branches of the Wentworth family and the construction of two of the finest mansions and numerous follies ever constructed in England, is explained in Chapter Six. Some reconstruction work on Wentworth Woodhouse may have commenced before the death of Thomas Watson Wentworth in 1723. His only son, Thomas Wentworth, succeeded him and he was a prolific builder. He also received a considerable number of honours, being created a Knight of the Bath in 1725, Baron Malton in 1628, Baron of Harowden, Viscount Higham and Earl of Malton in 1733. In 1746 he inherited the title Baron Rockingham from a cousin and later that same year was created Marquess of Rockingham. It was the first Marquess who was largely responsible for the rebuilding of Wentworth Woodhouse. The 130 ft central block of what is now the West or Garden Front (or Back Front, as local people refer to it) was constructed against what remains of the 17th-century house, which stretches beyond it to the south. The heraldic devices commemorating the bestowing of the Knighthood of the Bath on Thomas Wentworth, dates the work to before 1728. The architect for this Baroque front is not known, but it is believed to have been a follower of Sir John Vanbrugh. Suggestions for possible architects have included William Wakefield and William Etty of York. By 1734 work had been completed on this Baroque front, which has no rivals in England, this west-facing range being similar in design to buildings found in Austria or Bohemia. The building of the East Front had already commenced. During this period the name of the house was changed from Wentworth Woodhouse to Wentworth House. This postcard view of the West Front, published by Lichie Walker in the early 1920s, shows that old names do indeed die hard, as the caption says Wentworth House, a name which had officially not been used for at least 140 years, the house having reverted to its original name in the 1780s. *(Walker's Newsagents collection)*

Originally an entirely different style of architecture had been envisaged for the East Front, but the heroic Vanbrughian style which Lord Malton had chosen was already considered out of date by the time work on the West Front was nearing completion. His Lordship consulted Lord Burlington, considered to be the arbiter of fashion at that time, who recommended Henry Flitcroft (known as Burlington's Harry) as a suitable architect for the work, and suggested Wanstead House, designed by Colen Campbell for Sir Richard Childe in 1715 (demolished 1828), as a model on which to base it. Flitcroft designed the central portion of the East Front in the Palladian style, closely resembling Wanstead House, allowing his resident architect Ralph Tunnicliffe of Dalton to carry out work on the north and south wings. Flitcroft also designed the pavilions. A massive 1500 ft terrace was constructed with a bastion at the east end. Ralph Tunnicliffe supervised the work, which had a number of set-backs, for which Tunnicliffe was held responsible. The terrace was considered so important in the overall scheme that the interruption in its construction resulted in a delay in building the East Front. Tunnicliffe died in 1736 and Flitcroft took charge of the building project. The Earl of Malton wrote: 'In the Year 1737 the new Parlor and Drawing Room below Stairs were finished furnished and used, the Great Hall and Portico begun, the Cellars, Rustick Story compleated and the Great Hall erected to the Heigth of the first Window. . . . 1738 The Great Supping Room finished, the Place for a Stair Case erected. . . . 1739 The great Porticoe was built which considering the Size of the Stones and the Quantity of Carving etc was the greatest piece of Building I had ever done in one year. . . . 1740 the Two Windows joyning to the great Hall Northward were built and the supping room was first used and the rooms over it were wainscotted and the Cieling Joyce put into severall of the Rooms, also the Carving of the Arms and the other Ornaments of the great Front. . . . 1741 and 1742 The old Gallery was rebuilt, and the North Wing erected . . . the Carpenter's Work of the Ceilings of the Great Hall, Dining Room and Portico were finished and a rough Coat of Plaister laid on. . . . 1743 the new Gallery was fitted up and the masonry of the whole House, except some of the Ornaments, Paving etc. finished.' The portico takes up nine of the centre block's nineteen bays. Six giant Corinthian columns support the pediment, its entablature adorned with the Rockingham motto *Mea Gloria Fides*, My Faith is My Glory, and the tympanum with the arms of the Marquess of Rockingham. This 18th-century engraving shows the central portion of the East Front of Wentworth House. (*Author's collection*)

During the years that followed many fine craftsmen were engaged to work on the magnificent interior. Henry Flitcroft's most important contribution was the fitting out of seven rooms on the piano nobile, including his finest work, the Marble Saloon. The Marquess kept detailed accounts and records that show the millions of bricks that were made on the estate, stone which came from Hooton Roberts and glass from Bolsterstone Glass Works. By 1750, the year the First Marquess died, Wentworth Park had been extended to over 9 miles in circumference. Shortly before his death he wrote to his son and heir with the words of advice: 'If you lay out your money in improving your seat, lands, gardens etc. you beautifye the country and do the work ordered by God himself.' By his own reckoning Lord Rockingham had spent £82,500 over the previous quarter of a century, improving his house and grounds at Wentworth. Building on the great house continued. The new Marquess was his father's fifth, youngest and only surviving son, Charles, second Marquess of Rockingham, who was Prime Minister twice, firstly in 1765–6 and in 1782, when he died in office. Lord Rockingham married an heiress from Sheffield, Mary Bright, in 1752, but the marriage was childless. Like his father before him, the second Marquess made several major contributions to building on the estate; the most important was when he engaged Carr of York to design and build a stable block for eighty-four horses, in 1768: these were described as the finest stables in England. Lord Rockingham was an enthusiastic and influential patron of the turf and commissioned the greatest of all animal painters, George Stubbs, to paint some of his finest works. He also had two follies constructed, Lady's Folly and Keppel's Column, two of which remain popular landmarks to this day. On Lord Rockingham's death the estates passed to a son of his sister, William, fourth Earl Fitzwilliam; she had married the third Earl Fitzwilliam of Milton. Lord Fitzwilliam inherited estates from his uncle with an income of £40,000 a year. Between 1782 and 1784 John Carr designed alterations to Tunnicliffe's wing on Lord Fitzwilliam's instructions, in order to provide additional bedroom accommodation, principally for the domestic staff. The appearance of the East Front today owes much to Carr's efforts. The wings were originally one and a half storeys high and had plain broad pediments. Carr increased their height by adding an additional storey, reduced the pediment to three bays and added giant Corinthian columns. He also increased the height of the quadrants linking the wings to Flitcroft's end pavilions. When one compares the engraving of how the East Front appeared before 1784 with photographs of the house in more recent times, Carr's alterations can be clearly seen. The old name Wentworth Woodhouse came into use again during the time of the fourth Earl Fitzwilliam, who was himself a distinguished Whig politician. Surprisingly, even though the name Wentworth House was used for only a little over fifty years, many locals still refer to it by that name. This 18th-century engraving was specially produced for *The Modern Universal British Traveller*. (*Author's collection*)

Work continued on the fitting out of the rooms until the early 1800s. Lord Fitzwilliam engaged Humphrey Repton to landscape Wentworth Park in 1790. Repton noted that the extensive park had very few trees, the house being surrounded by 'coarse grass and boulders'. He began by taking down four obelisks from the garden, then removed boulders from the meadows, which he returfed to form lawns. An extensive earth-moving operation followed, to round and soften the contours of the land. Two large pools visible from the East Front were transformed into a serpentine lake, and a large number of trees were planted. Wentworth Park was considered to be one of Repton's most successful transformations. However, much of Repton's great work of art was destroyed by opencast mining, despite a passionate speech in the House of Lords by the eighth Earl Fitzwilliam in an attempt to prevent this compulsory destruction. The first stage of this unnecessary act of institutionalised vandalism was carried out between 1946 and 1947, and instigated by Emmanuel Shinwell, the Minister of Fuel and Power in Attlee's Labour government. In this first stage 132,000 tons of coal were taken out from the gardens proper. Then the NCB open-cast mined the park between the East Front and the Mausoleum in a massive programme of work between 1956 and 1961. This time 370,000 tons of top-grade coal was obtained. Precautions were taken to stop the lakes silting up and attempts were made to reinstate the park, including the re-planting of 3 acres of Repton's woodland, which had been completely destroyed. Although Wentworth Park is very attractive, it is unlikely it will ever be as beautiful as it was in the 1940s. This is the Stable Block, 1920s. *(Walker's Newsagents collection)*

The East Front of Wentworth Woodhouse from a Lichie Walker postcard, 1920s. Not so much a house but one of the finest palaces in Europe, it has more than one boast. It is effectively three houses in one, the home of the Earls of Strafford being sandwiched between the buildings constructed by the Rockinghams. Wentworth Woodhouse is the largest private house in the United Kingdom (the second largest being Knole, the home of the Sackvilles, situated near Sevenoaks in Kent). The East Front at 606 ft is the longest of any country house in England. Its interiors were designed by some of the most renowned craftsmen and artists ever to have worked in England. In 1808, Earl Fitzwilliam prefixed the surname of Wentworth to his own. (*Walker's Newsagents collection*)

The Fitzwilliam (Grove) hounds, 1920s. With the combined fortunes of the Wentworth, Watson Wentworth, Bright and Fitzwilliam families, the Wentworth Fitzwilliams became one of the wealthiest families in the land. The family was known for its benevolence towards estate workers, miners, foundry workers and the like, and provided superior living accommodation in Wentworth and elsewhere on the estate to house them. On 13 May 1948 the eighth Earl Fitzwilliam, who had inherited the title on the death of his father in 1944, was killed in an air crash at the age of 37. He had a daughter but no direct male heir. The ninth Earl was a cousin of the seventh Earl, and was 65 when he inherited the title. His marriage had ended in divorce and there were no children. He died on 3 April 1952. Death duties on the Fitzwilliam estates were enormous, and as three heads of the family had died in less than ten years meant that considerable economies had to be made. The new earl, the tenth, affectionately known as Lord Tom by the locals, was the fifth Earl Fitzwilliam's great grandson, and had inherited the Fitzwilliam Milton Estate by descent from his father. (*George Hardy collection*)

In 1953 the stable block and a substantial part of Wentworth Woodhouse, including the whole of the East Front, were leased to the West Riding County Council on a long-term care and maintenance lease. It was opened as the Lady Mabel College, named in honour of Lady Mabel Smith, a granddaughter of the sixth Earl and sister of the seventh Earl, who was a Labour County Councillor in the West Riding and later a county Alderman. She died in 1951. The family continued to use the principal part of the West Front at certain times of year. On the death of the tenth Earl in 1979 the title became extinct. The remaining contents of Wentworth Woodhouse were inherited by the daughter of the eighth Earl. Lady Mabel College, originally a teacher training college of physical education for ladies, was engulfed by Sheffield Polytechnic in 1977, which took a sub-lease. In 1986 the Wentworth Woodhouse site was abandoned completely, leaving the Metropolitan Borough of Rotherham with an expensive repair and maintenance lease, inherited from the defunct West Riding County Council. The Well Gate, situated in Chapel Court, dates from the great Earl of Strafford's time. *(George Hardy collection)*

The East Front of Wentworth Woodhouse, July 1999. Plans to turn this Grade I listed building into a luxury hotel were turned down. Then in 1989 Wentworth Woodhouse, the stable block, college buildings and a few acres of land immediately surrounding it, were sold to the reclusive multi-millionaire Wensley Haydon-Bailley. The owners of the estate, the heirs of the eighth and tenth Earls, felt that he was best placed to secure the future of the house. He later purchased the freehold and some additional land. Ambitious plans simply didn't happen. In 1998 Haydon-Bailley went spectacularly bust and the Wentworth Woodhouse site, including about 80 acres of land, was put up for sale by the mortgagee, the Swiss bank Julius Baer & Co. The price asked for what is considered to be one of the finest palaces in Europe was ludicrously low, £1,500,000. The asking price represented just £7 per square foot, compared with £70 per square foot being asked for a terraced house in nearby Rotherham. In June 1999 it was announced that Wentworth Woodhouse has been sold to Mr Clifford Newbold, a 72-year-old retired architect from Highgate, North London. He has several business interests and is listed as Company Secretary of Burlington Homes. He intends to live there with numerous family members. *(Author's commission)*

The gardens of Wentworth Woodhouse are situated to the west of the mansion. Wentworth Garden Centre occupies the site of the kitchen gardens, the Japanese Garden, the Blue Garden, the site of the great glasshouses, the maze and conservatory lawn; one can begin to appreciate exactly what this more secluded area meant to the residents of the great house. Good close-up views of the East Front were readily available, but views of the West Front were restricted. There is still a considerable amount of land which separates the West Front from the Garden Centre. Maud, Countess Fitzwilliam, was responsible for creating the Japanese Garden during the early 1900s and this has been partially restored to its former glory, with the celebrated 'Bear Pit' dating from the 17th century forming an unusual focal point. Many of the other features date back to the early years of the 19th century and some to the 18th century. The following postcard views of various parts of the gardens were published by Lichie Walker in the 1920s. The Camelia House shown here remains in the private gardens belonging to the new owner of the mansion. *(Walker's Newsagents collection)*

A view from the Camelia House across the Rose Garden to the Rotunda, which lies at the southern end of the Great Terrace. *(Walker's Newsagents collection)*

The Blue Garden Terrace. *(Walker's Newsagents collection)*

The maze, described on the postcard as Puzzle Garden. *(Walker's Newsagents collection)*

The Palm House, situated in one of the great glasshouses, now demolished. *(Walker's Newsagents collection)*

A composite postcard published by Lichie Walker of Wentworth Woodhouse and gardens. *(Walker's Newsagents collection)*

There are various lodges dotted around the park and the estate, some of which are very grand. North Lodge was, as the name suggests, built on the northern fringe of Wentworth Park. Granny Clarke, the lodge-keeper, is shown here on her 83rd birthday in 1905. The barred gate opposite leads directly up to The Needle's Eye. *(George Hardy collection)*

Rainborough Lodge, popularly known as Lions Lodge because of the two lions standing sentinel on the gateposts. The lodge marks the path of the straight roadway which runs up to The Needle's Eye. This postcard view is incorrectly titled Lyons Lodge, West Melton. *(George Hardy collection)*

Of the four major monuments on the Fitzwilliam Wentworth Estate, The Needle's Eye is the smallest and oldest. Its true origin or purpose will probably never be known. There is a widely held local belief that it was built in 1780, when the Marquess of Rockingham bet that he could drive a coach and four through the eye of a needle. This myth may have been popularised in the early 20th century, when locals added spice to the stories about the monument's origins, which may have been fuelled during the First World War when the seventh Earl Fitzwilliam drove a gun carriage through The Needle's Eye. However, what is certain is that The Needle's Eye is shown in pictorial form on a plan of the estate of the Earl of Malton in 1746 (the year Lord Malton was elevated to the marquisate); and a document listing building expenses between 1722 and 1723 refers to 'an obelisk in Lee Wood'. This is probably the first documentary mention of The Needle's Eye.

The striking monument tops a ridge at the edge of Lee Wood and is situated about two-thirds of a mile from Wentworth Woodhouse. It is the least noticeable of the major monuments on the estate but there are several vantage points from which it can be viewed. It is a pyramid standing about 45 ft high and pierced by a gothic ogee arch, constructed of ashlar blocks hewn from local sandstone and surmounted by a large ornamental urn. There is a stone seat built into the walls of the arch. A private road which originally ran from the great house to Rainborough Lodge passes through The Needle's Eye. Looking southwards from the monument towards North Lodge, one can clearly see the road cutting through the trees of Lee Wood. It is a rather romantic sight, the old roadway covered in woodland foliage whatever the season. Looking northwards, the fields through which the roadway passed have been ploughed over many times. It is still possible to see a gap in the trees marking the road's route to Rainborough Lodge, and at certain times of year a broad stripe can be clearly seen in the ground, marking the line of the road across the fields. Another local legend is that the road continued from Rainborough Lodge to Doncaster Racecourse. This may have sprung from the fact that the second Marquess of Rockingham was a great patron of the turf.

The Needle's Eye was in such a state of disrepair by the late 1960s that there was great concern for its future. Fortunately it was expertly repaired, and is now in the care of the Fitzwilliam Amenity Trust. (*George Hardy collection*)

Hoober Stand is an exceptional structure. This extraordinary-looking building is the most prominent and best-known monument on the Fitzwilliam Wentworth Estate. It can be seen from all directions, and is situated on the loftiest ridge in the locality on the same contour line as The Needle's Eye, which lies about 1½ miles to its west. Its base stands at 518 ft above sea level, one of the highest points in the South Yorkshire area, and its position coupled with its striking appearance makes it one of the most famous landmarks in the West Riding.

Hoober Stand takes its name from the hamlet of Hoober and the hill where it is situated. It was built to commemorate the suppression of the Jacobite Rebellion in 1745. A marble tablet above the doorway has this inscription: '1748. This Pyramidall Building was Erected by His MAJESTY'S most Dutyfull Subject THOMAS, Marquess of Rockingham etc. In Grateful respect to the Preserver of our Religion Laws and Libertys KING GEORGE the Second. Who, by the Blessing of God, having subdued a most Unnatural Rebellion in Britain Anno 1746 Maintains the Ballance of Power and Settles a Just and Honourable Peace in Europe 1748.' It is more likely that the Marquess was paying homage to his monarch from a more personal level. For in 1746 Thomas Watson Wentworth, Earl of Malton, was further ennobled by being created Marquess of Rockingham. The Earl of Malton, as Lord Lieutenant of Yorkshire, served in 1745 under the Duke of Cumberland, who finally routed the Jacobites at Culloden in 1746. It was for these services that his elevation took place.

Henry Flitcroft was engaged as architect. Here he strayed from the rigid Palladian correctness of his other works, including the east front of Wentworth Woodhouse. In Hoober Stand he created something quite remarkable. This three-sided structure would have been unusual had the walls been straight, but three sided and sloping makes Hoober Stand unique.

Work started in 1747 and the entire project was completed in 1749. The cupola rises to 90 ft, and according to Dr Richard Pococke, who travelled through the district in 1750, recording his observations, York Minister, some 40 miles distant, is visible from the platform. This is one of the most extraordinary buildings ever built in England. It is geometrically perfect, but because of a clever trick it appears to be falling down, whichever way you look at it. Either by accident or design, Flitcroft has created a monumental masterpiece. From a distance it is majestic, but close to, Flitcroft's breathtaking design gives one the impression that tons of masonry are about to fall on one's head. From any angle the domed cupola appears to be off centre, again because of Flitcroft's tricks with symmetry.

Hoober Stand is an 80 ft high sloping pyramid which ends in a corbelled parapet. Crowning this is a hexagonal domed cupola positioned directly above the central staircase. There are sundials in each corner of the platform. Five round-arched and pedimented windows light the staircase. The base of the monument measures 42 ft, and 155 steps wind their way to the top.

In 1879 lightning struck Hoober Stand and a window was damaged. Because of concerns that the monument was unsafe, it has remained closed to the public for many years. In 1992 some minor restoration took place, when badly eroded stones around the door were replaced and the plaque above the doorway was replaced by a replica. As I write this in August 1999 a complete restoration is in progress.

Because of its prominent position, fireworks and bonfires were not unusual at Hoober Stand. Many events were celebrated there. In 1887 fireworks and feasting marked the Golden Wedding of the sixth Earl and Countess Fitzwilliam, and in 1931 the coming of age of Viscount Milton was celebrated in great style. Hoober Stand is owned by the Fitzwilliam Amenity Trust. (George Hardy collection)

Keppel's Column, near Rotherham

Keppel's Column, seen here in about 1900, is situated at what was originally the southern edge of Wentworth Park. This gigantic column is now in a semi-urban setting, and although striking in appearance it is less well known than Hoober Stand. Some locals refer to the column as 'Scholes Skoppy' and others 'Scholes Cappice', and these names have been used for generations. It is clear where the confusion in the name arises. Keppel's Column towers above the nearby Scholes Coppice and an ancient fort, situated down the slope from the column, on the southern edge of the park. Scholes Coppice is today severely depleted in size, as its trees originally came almost to the foot of the column, but the close proximity of the column and the relative inaccessibility of the latter, and also the fact that all three landmarks lie on rising ground above the hamlet of Scholes, has clearly led to this confusion of names.

How Keppel's Column came into being is most interesting. The second Marquess of Rockingham decided he wanted a landscape feature to the south of his residence, which could be seen from the East Front. Work began in 1773. It cannot be determined exactly when Lord Rockingham approached John Carr, the eminent Yorkshire architect, for suggested designs, but he had been associated with His Lordship since 1753. The monument was not conceived in its present form, and over the eight years or so it took to complete the design changed several times. It is possible that Carr was commissioned to design the monument after Lord Rockingham had changed his mind on its form, but no documents have yet appeared to confirm this. In 1773 work began on 'Scholes Pyramid'. Then his lordship decided that one of the obelisks from the garden be used in the design, as he had felt somewhat deflated and I dare say mildly insulted when Horace Walpole, the self-appointed arbiter of national taste, described the garden as a nine-pin bowling alley, because of the abundance of obelisks to be found there. The idea was that one obelisk should be placed on a 45 ft high tower. John Hobson, the mason, made an estimate of £115 3s 0d for this work.

By 1776, it is clear the Marquess had changed his mind again, for the tower and obelisk had become a column and he requested a revised estimate. An estimate was prepared 'of ye Expence of raising ye Column in Scholes Spring 78 feet higher than it now is on ye above Date & fitting a stone Ballistrade and Coping above the Top platform'. On a map showing the estate in 1788 the monument is marked as 'Scholes Column'. Exactly when work was halted and the column modified, resulting in the re-alignment of the curve, is not clear, but evidence indicates that it was sometime after the decision had been taken to commemorate Admiral Keppel. The ancient Greeks were the first to realise the optical illusion that columns with straight sides do not appear to be straight at all: the entasis (or curve) was mathematically calculated to give the appearance of straightness. In the case of Keppel's Column, Carr worked out the curve for a taller column, and the result of the shortening of the height of the finished structure can clearly be seen. What is apparent is the stage the building work was at when the Marquess decided to curtail the height of the column. The top 40 ft, almost a third of the total height, was the minimum amount which could preserve the curve and finish off the column as neatly as possible, which means that the column had reached the height of about 75 ft when the instruction was given to finish the column. So, instead of the intended 150 ft, which would have been the correct height in relation to the curve, Keppel's Column stands 115 ft. Carr clearly had to severely adjust the design in order that the effect would not be too visually unappealing, and he just about gets away with it; even so, the result of this re-alignment is that the column bulges dramatically and the effect is startling. To the casual passer-by the column just doesn't seem quite right, but exactly why is puzzling. *(George Hardy collection)*

Keppel's Column from the north, 1999. The building of Keppel's Column took a long time, and the Marquess became fired with enthusiasm to give the column a political meaning. A turn of events finally gave him the excuse he needed to complete the monument. His friend and ally Admiral Keppel was court martialled on a charge of misconduct and neglect of duty. Lord Rockingham was incensed by this, and lent his support to Keppel wholeheartedly. A petition in Keppel's defence was signed by twelve admirals. The charges were dismissed as 'malicious and unfounded', and Keppel's acquittal on 11 February 1779 was the occasion for great rejoicing. It caused embarrassment to the ruling Tory party, with suggestions of corruption in the highest places.

The Marquess instructed his steward 'to have Wentworth House illuminated (that part which you think most proper), the Guns fired, a Hogshead of Ale to be given away to the populace, and such other demonstrations of Joy as you think necessary on the Occasion'. As many as 10,000 people are said to have gathered in front of the great house to celebrate the event. Lord Rockingham was delighted at the embarrassment caused to the King and 'his' party, and this caused him to reconsider the design of the Great Column. He originally intended to commemorate his friend's acquittal with a more lavish monument than the one he eventually settled on. He envisaged a statue of Keppel on top of the column and a ship's prow at each corner of the base, but after even more compromises the plans were never fully implemented.

Keppel's Column stands on a square base, which measures 23 ft across. The column is exceedingly plain and is of the Tuscan order, being 17 ft in diameter and 136 ft high, according to Carr, with a cap and base of ashlar and a shaft of square coursed rubble, pierced with small openings which light a spiral stair. Carr may have included the massive base in his measurements, because the official height of the column is given at 115 ft, but add the base, cap and railings and this may well add up to 136 ft. The great flat ashlar slab which tops the column is not quite square, being 17 ft 6 in by 16 ft 6 in. A plain iron balustrade crowns the top of the monument. There are 217 steps to the top of Keppel's Column and 21 small staircase windows light the way. Unfortunately it is no longer possible to climb the steps to the top of the column, as they are considered unsafe. The view from the base of the column looking northwards across the park is one to be savoured; from the top of the column the views all around must be stupendous. Keppel's Column is now in the care of Rotherham MBC. It has been rumoured that there are distant hopes of restoring this important monument and opening it to the public. Keppel's Column can be seen from many miles around. There is a good view of the column from the M1 motorway, where it dominates the skyline. It is a great shame that this magnificent monument remains inaccessible. (*Author's commission*)

The Mausoleum is the most recent of the four major monuments on the Fitzwilliam Wentworth Estate. It is also the only one which needs to be viewed at close quarters to appreciate it fully, as only the cupola can be seen protruding above the treetops in the middle of the wood that surrounds it. From an architectural point of view it is the most pleasing to the eye, and is certainly the most important. In the real sense of the word it is not a mausoleum at all, as it contains no human remains, nor has it ever. In reality, it could more accurately be described as a cenotaph, the literal meaning of which is a monument to one whose remains are elsewhere. However, it stands as a memorial to a man who was much lamented at his death and whom his grateful nephew saw fit to commemorate.

The Mausoleum was erected by William, fourth Earl Fitzwilliam, in memory of his uncle, the second Marquess of Rockingham, who is buried in York Minster. His nephew felt that a fitting memorial should be erected nearer his home. Pevsner calls it 'an outstandingly fine and noble structure'. Joseph Hunter commented in 1831: 'As few noblemen ever went to the grave carrying with them more of the respect of their families, their friends, and their country, so few are commemorated by so superb a memorial as that which the piety of Earl Fitzwilliam raised to the memory of his friend, relative and benefactor.'

John Carr was appointed as architect to design and build the monument. Building began in 1784 and took four years to complete, using ten men. Carr produced several designs for the mausoleum. The design opted for was one resembling the Roman tomb of the Julii at St Remy in Provence. There is a portrait of the St Remy monuments hanging in the dining room at Rokeby. This was one of the pictures collected by Sir Thomas Robins and was bought with the house in 1769 by J.S. Morritt. As Carr carried out work for Mr Morritt, it seems likely that he was familiar with the painting, which may have been his inspiration for the mausoleum in Wentworth Park. In any event, Carr's masterpiece is nearly twice the size of the mausoleum in Provence. Carr created a three-storey building, some 90 ft high. The ground floor is a solid, square structure, built of ashlar blocks in the local sandstone. It has a pedimented entrance supported by two columns of the Tuscan order. Above is an open colonnade supported by Corinthian columns, which contains an empty sarcophagus. The entire structure is surmounted by a cupola which is designed to resemble a Roman temple. Four large vases ornamented with veined and carved leaves are sited at the corners of the penultimate storey. Within the mausoleum is a life-size statue, in marble, by Nollekens of the Marquess in garter robes, with upraised hand. On the base is an inscription in prose by Edmund Burke, and in verse by Frederick Montagu. The interior is magnificently delicate and light. It is reminiscent of the finest Adam drawing room. The outer walls of the ground floor chamber afford further delights. There are eight busts of Rockingham's 'Whig' luminaries placed in niches. The originals, also by Nollekens, were removed and are now at Bourne Park, Kent, home of Lady Juliet Tadgell, daughter of the eighth Earl Fitzwilliam; but they have been replaced by plaster casts of outstanding quality. The busts are of Edmund Burke, Charles James Fox, Admiral Viscount Keppel, John Lee, Lord John Cavendish, the Duke of Portland, Frederick Montagu and Sir George Saville.

The building was enclosed by a fence of 743 railings made by the Rotherham iron founders Samuel Walker and Company. In 1792, during the time Humphrey Repton was landscaping Wentworth Park, the four large obelisks standing 50 ft high, which had adorned the garden of the west front of Wentworth Woodhouse, were removed. They were placed inside the enclosure of the mausoleum, and a large number of trees were planted on the surrounding hillside. The account book for the construction of the Rockingham Mausoleum runs to twenty-eight pages. It records the cost of building materials, as well as payments to local craftsmen and to Carr, the architect, and Nollekens, the sculptor. The total amount recorded is £3,208 3s 4d. (Chris Thawley collection)

There is a story concerning the mausoleum which has been told for many years. When the statue of the Marquess of Rockingham was unveiled, someone present pointed out to the sculptor that it was a perfect likeness, apart from a row of stitching which had been omitted from his lordship's garter robes. The sculptor was so distraught on hearing this that he committed suicide. It is just a story, though, which I have heard told by several locals. Joseph Nollekens (1737–1823) was one of the most gifted sculptors of that period. Small in stature, he was known as 'Little Nolly'. Despite amassing a fortune, which on his death amounted to £200,000, he and his wife were noted for their parsimony. There was hardly anyone of note who was not portrayed by him. He knew and mixed with all the great people of his time, yet despite his undoubted genius as a sculptor it was said that in talk and behaviour he was 'little more than one remove from an idiot', and lived in Mortimer Street, London, in what was described by those who knew him as circumstances of unequalled squalor. He wished to die as he

had lived – a miser, expressing in his will that 'my body be decently deposited in the vault under the parish church of Paddington . . . in a plain black coffin without any gilt ornaments'.

For several years, this Grade I listed building was clad in an ugly metal jacket, to save it from the ravages of mining subsidence. In his book of reminiscences, *A Glance over my Shoulder*, Clarence Walker remembers: 'Around 1950 I was in charge of the exploration of the foundations of the Mausoleum. We had to take up some of the flagstones leading to the monument. We had orders that on no account must we break a flagstone, which proved to be a most difficult task since we found the flagstones were dove-tailed together and run with lead. However we finally succeeded and then dug a trench to the foundation. Here we found a tunnel all round with an outer wall. I was able to creep all around the foundations, which proved to be inadequate for the support of such a large edifice. The purpose of this exercise was to ascertain what measures were needed to protect the building until coal had been extracted from under the foundations.' Following the closure of the last remaining coal mines in the area, and the subsequent withdrawal of the threat of damage by severe earth movements, the jacket has now been removed. With the aid of grants from British Coal and English Heritage, it has been possible to remove the iron clamps which have kept the monument stable. The mausoleum is the property of the Fitzwilliam Amenity Trust, whose trustees have opened this magnificent architectural and historic gem to the public. *(George Hardy collection)*

Main Street, Wentworth, early 1920s. Very little has changed in almost eighty years. *(Walker's Newsagents collection)*

One of Wentworth's two former windmills, photographed in the first quarter of the 20th century. This one lies in open countryside, topping the ridge between Wentworth and Harley. *(Chris Thawley collection)*

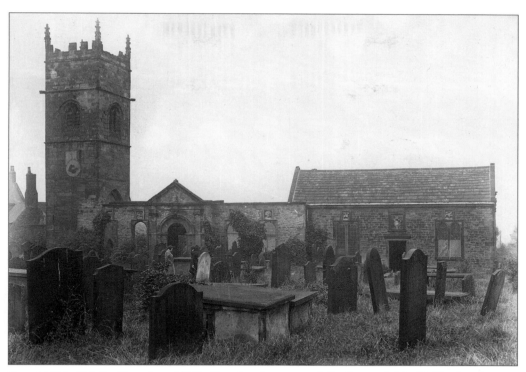

The old Holy Trinity Church, *c. 1920*. The church was partially dismantled in 1877 after the new Holy Trinity Church opened. *(Walker's Newsagents collection)*

Wentworth Battery Territorial Army, *c. 1917*. Back row, left to right: Jim Swift, John W. Bell, George Jackson, -?-. Front row: George West, -?-, -?-. *(George Hardy collection)*

The new church of the Holy Trinity, consecrated on 31 July 1877, and seen here in the early 1920s. It was built in memory of their parents by the children of the fifth Earl Fitzwilliam. The east window was installed in memory of Countess Harriet, wife of the sixth Earl, who died in 1895. The church was designed by that great exponent of Gothic Revival J.L. Pearson, whose other work includes Truro Cathedral and Cliveden, home of the Astor family. *(Walker's Newsagents collection)*

CHAPTER FIVE

TANKERSLEY & PILLEY

Tankersley (including Tankersley Park) and the village of Pilley are closely connected. Both are mentioned in the Domesday Survey of 1086. Pilley is the larger settlement, whereas Tankersley gives its name to the parish. Tanchere or Thancred, from which the name is derived, was the first Saxon lord in the area, the ley or 'leah' part denoting a meadow, lea or woodland clearing. During the reign of Edward the Confessor Ledwin, its lord, paid taxes of about 20s. There was a church and a priest, woodland pasture 1 square mile in extent, as well as farmland. The population was around thirty souls and by the time the Normans had laid waste the area its value had greatly decreased to a taxable value of just 7s.

The church mentioned in the Domesday Survey is believed to have been built by three Saxon lords, Ledwin of Tankersley, Ulsi of Wortley and Elric of Pilley, during the 10th century. Ledwin was dispossessed and his lands given by William the Conqueror to his half-brother Robert, Count de Mortain. In 1088 he was banished from the kingdom and his land restored to his son William, who also fell foul of the king during the reign of Henry I.

In 1187 the church of St Peter was built at Tankersley. A manor house with a moat surrounding it was erected nearby. Today Glebe Farm (so called because glebeland was farmland set aside for the support of the local clergyman and his church) and the former rectory (built in 1870) occupy the site. The remains of the moat can still be seen. The de Tankersley family were living in the manor house in the 12th century and remained there until the death of Sir Richard de Tankersley in 1290, when his daughters Joan and Alice succeeded him. Joan's husband, Hugh de Eland, obtained a royal warrant to hunt deer in Tankersley in 1303, resulting in Tankersley Park being enclosed in 1303–4. The area at the edge of Tankersley Park, just within the present-day Sheffield conurbation, known as Warren, takes its name from that period, because the name Warren has its origins in the keeping of a deer park. The boundaries of the 12th century enclosure can still be followed along 4½ miles of footpaths, hedges and walls, the eastern boundary of which is the old turnpike running from Hoyland Common into Chapeltown. The population of Tankersley had gradually increased, and by this time a plentiful supply of fresh meat was required. Medieval lords ensured that by building dovecotes (doves and pigeons being a major contributor of meat in the winter diet), setting aside land for rabbits and hares and by enclosing deer parks. The park was a major economic asset, with fishponds and woodland, as well as providing sport.

During the reign of Richard II Isabel, daughter and heiress of Thomas Eland, married Sir John Saville. The poll tax return of 1379 shows that the population of Tankersley had increased to 110. The manor of Tankersley continued in the Savilles' control until the reign of James I. In about 1546 they built Tankersley Lodge, which soon became known as Tankersley Hall. This became the principal mansion on the estate, when the former manor house became a farm, which was eventually demolished and replaced by another. The Savilles sold the estate and it changed hands again, until in 1631 Viscount Wentworth (later the First Earl of Strafford) purchased it from Philip, Earl of Pembroke, for £4,500. It has remained in the ownership of the Wentworth, or as it is now known, the Fitzwilliam Wentworth Estate ever since. Lord Wentworth extended the park, drained the marshy areas and cleaned out the fishponds, but he gave the estate less attention than its previous owners as he didn't live in the hall, preferring to reside at his ancestral seat at Wentworth, 2 miles to the east. In 1635 His Lordship appointed his cousin Rockley 'Master of the Game at Tankersley Park' and charged him with maintaining the lodge, increasing the red deer to about 280, and restocking the fishponds. Civil War erupted in 1642, and a minor battle took place on Tankersley Moor. Some of the Royalist Duke of Newcastle's men met enemy forces on Tankersley Moor. The Royalists won the day and many Roundheads were slain or taken prisoner.

The last recorded occupants of Tankersley Lodge or Hall were Sir Richard Fanshaw and his family. Fanshaw's occupancy came about because of his connection with the Wentworth family. In 1640 he was made secretary to the Council of War under the Earl of Strafford in Ireland. In 1644 he became Secretary for War under the Prince of Wales, then aged 14. While Sir Richard was on business for the Prince in Paris, Charles I was executed. Sir Richard remained loyal to the Royalist cause and fought in the Battle of Worcester, where he was wounded and taken prisoner. He was imprisoned in the Tower of London, then moved to Whitehall, where he was kept under close arrest. He was seriously ill and was bailed for £4,000 in order to have medical treatment. In 1653 he was allowed to go to Bath to receive this. That winter he went to visit his friend William, second Earl of Strafford, at Wentworth Woodhouse. Lord Strafford offered Sir Richard Tankersley Hall as a temporary residence, and in 1653 Sir Richard took a twenty-one year lease on Tankersley Park. He moved there with Lady Fanshaw and three children in that spring. On parole, he was not permitted to travel more than 5 miles from his new home without special leave.

The lease which was drawn up between Lord Strafford and Sir Richard indicates that Lord Strafford was contemplating extracting iron and coal in and around Tankersley Park, including the erection of 'Iron Mills'. A survey conducted in 1772 for the second Marquess of Rockingham shows that both coal and ironstone had been worked within a field's length of the hall. The accompanying map drawn up by the surveyor, William Fairbanks, shows the ruins of Tankersley Old Hall and indicates where land had been worked and where mining was taking place. It is clear that the twenty-one year lease signed by Sir Richard was an ideal arrangement for Lord Strafford, because while the surface working took place it was unlikely that another suitable tenant could have been found. Sir Richard and Lady Fanshaw's stay at Tankersley Hall did not last long. In 1654 their daughter, Ann, contracted smallpox and died. She was buried in a vault in the nearby St Peter's Church. Sir Richard and his family went to stay with Lady Fanshaw's sister at Hamerton in Huntingdonshire. In a pictorial survey conducted between 1723 and 1728 Tankersley Hall is shown intact, with its outbuildings in good condition and red deer in the park. Daniel Defoe visited Tankersley Park in 1727, and stated that the red deer were the biggest in Europe. Sometime between then and 1772 the hall became sufficiently dilapidated to be described as a ruin.

The second Marquess of Rockingham adapted Tankersley Park to suit the more refined taste of the second half of the 18th century. He planted trees, created artificial lakes and built Lady's Folly, a Grecian-style retreat. Towards the end of the century further mining took place in Tankersley Park and the beginning of the Industrial Revolution saw its devastation. Ironstone and coal mining ravaged the countryside between Hood Hill and Pilley Hills. The land in between, Tankersley Park, Westwood and Upper Tankersley, were worked until there was nothing left to extract. Shallow bell pits were dug by miners working alongside the ruined hall. (Today the slag heaps which were left behind provide the contours of Tankersley Golf Course.) In 1837 an inclined plane railway was built which took iron ore and coal from Tankersley Park to Elsecar Basin. The irregular holes left behind by bell pit mining rendered the land unfit for agricultural purposes. Trees were planted where woodland had not existed previously. Today the mature woods at Hood Hill, Bell Ground, Westwood and Upper Tankersley cover the sites where extensive mining once took place. The M1 motorway cuts a swathe through the centre of Tankersley Park, less than 100 yds from the ruins of Tankersley Old Hall, separating it from the golf course. It also cuts the parish of Tankersley in half, making communication between the two halves extremely difficult.

After the opening of the Wharncliffe Silkstone Colliery near Pilley in 1854 the influx of labour increased the population. In 1861, 1,403 people lived in the parish of Tankersley. Houses and cottages were built in Pilley to accommodate the new residents. For over a hundred years mines opened and closed but King Coal ruled the day, until the 1970s. Mines began to close for one reason or another, but no new mines opened. Wharncliffe Silkstone Colliery closed in 1971 and others followed. After the 1984 miners' strike, instigated by the proposed closure of Cortonwood Colliery, situated 4 miles from Tankersley, closures increased throughout South Yorkshire. There is no coal mining or iron ore mining taking place anywhere locally as the 20th century closes. In 1999 the parish of Tankersley consists of around 2,000 souls. The site of the former Wharncliffe Silkstone Colliery is now occupied by the Wentworth Industrial Estate. However, in comparison with the mine, employment prospects there for local people are very poor.

The Lady's Folly, Tankersley Park, seen here shortly before its demolition. It was built as a retreat for his wife Mary, Marchioness of Rockingham by Charles, the second Marquess, in the 1760s. This monument is the only major monument on the Fitzwilliam estate that has been demolished. By 1960 its structure had become severely dilapidated and was considered dangerous. If only it had survived another twenty years, I feel sure that in more conservation-minded times this building would have survived. A stone memorial records the building's existence. *(George Hardy collection)*

Tankersley Old Hall, 1920s. The hall was partially demolished in the 18th century to use as building stone for various buildings elsewhere on the estate. Fireplaces can still be seen in place in the interior walls. In the film *Kes* this was the location chosen in which to film David Bradley (later known as Dai Bradley), who played the character Billy Casper, scaling the walls to take a kestrel from its nest. *(Walker's Newsagents collection)*

St Peter's Church, Tankersley, *c. 1925*. The church replaced a Saxon church, part of the stonework of which has been incorporated in the 12th- and 13th-century parts of the present church. The tower is built in the Perpendicular style but with the exception of the late 16th-century clerestory and the north aisle, rebuilt in 1881, most of the rest of the church is built in the Decorated style. The chancel is the oldest intact part and dates from the period when the Eland family were lords of the manor. For centuries the incumbents had been appointed by the residents of the Manor House and later the Hall, and the parish of Tankersley was one of the richest livings in England. In the 18th century tithe records show that its income from tithes alone amounted to £1,000 annually. By the middle of the 20th century income had declined considerably. Much of the property owned by the living had been sold to fund repair projects, and with the nationalisation of the coal industry in 1947 mineral royalty payments ended. At the end of the 20th century the parish has a population of around 2,000, consisting mostly of retired mineworkers and their families. The church is still well attended. In the churchyard are buried many important industrialists from the 19th century, including Richard Hinchcliffe, Mineral Agent at the Tankersley mines and Assistant Agent to Earl Fitzwilliam (d. 1851), George Chambers (d. 1858), coal mine owner, Arthur Marshall Chambers (d. 1898) of the famous firm Newton Chambers, and numerous workers and officials connected with the ironstone and coal-mining industries. In the porch there are several inlaid slabs with crosses and swords and inside the church, near the pulpit, is a memorial to Ann Fanshaw, daughter of Sir Richard and Lady Fanshaw, Tankersley Hall's last occupants. Cannon balls from the battle of Tankersley Moor can be seen in a display case. (*Walker's Newsagents collection*)

Tankersley Welfare Hall, 1920s. *(Walker's Newsagents collection)*

The Children's Corner, Tankersley Welfare Hall, 1920s. *(Walker's Newsagents collection)*

Wentworth and Hoyland Common station decorated for the visit of their Majesties King George V and Queen Mary, July 1912. *(Edward Ellis collection)*

The turnpike which passes under the railway bridge at Wentworth and Hoyland Common station marks the boundary of Tankersley Park, which lies to the right. The booking office can be seen just past the bridge on the right, next to the detached station master's house, and row of cottages. The station opened in 1897 and closed on 2 November 1959. *(Edward Ellis collection)*

The Midland Railway Company Ambulance Stores at Wentworth and Hoyland Common station, *c.* 1910. *(Edward Ellis collection)*

A harvest festival at Warren Lane chapel, 1950s. *(Joan Hopson collection)*

Whitsuntide Celebrations, Warren Lane, *c.* 1953. In the scene are Miss Chapman, Miss Goddard, Katherine Hindley, Patricia Waite and front right, holding a bouquet of flowers, Carol Hopson. *(Joan Hopson collection)*

Cutting a swathe through Tankersley Park during the construction of the M1 motorway. *(Joan Masheder collection)*

CHAPTER SIX

WENTWORTH CASTLE & THE SURROUNDING VILLAGES

One of South Yorkshire's other great country houses, which also lies close to Hoyland, is the source of much confusion. Wentworth Castle is neither a castle, nor was it built at Wentworth. It was built 6 miles to the north-west of Wentworth Woodhouse. A superb long-distance view of this magnificent former home of the Wentworth family can be seen from Hoyland Law Stand, although the vista has been marred by the M1 motorway which cuts a swathe through the old park on its way north towards Barnsley and south towards Birdwell. The building of this beautiful largely Baroque mansion was a result of the rivalry which existed between two branches of the Wentworth family. Thomas Wentworth, second but first surviving son of Sir William Wentworth of Stanley Hall, Northgate Head, Wakefield, brother of the first Earl of Strafford, inherited the title Lord Raby, the Wentworth family's junior title, and also the baronetcy, on the death of the second Earl of Strafford in 1695. A rivalry developed between his branch of the family and the usurping Thomas Watson Wentworth of Wentworth Woodhouse, the chosen heir of the Wentworth estates. This new Lord Raby was deeply aggrieved at inheriting the title but not the ancestral home and estates. It was a sensational disposition, although perfectly legal, but it nevertheless divorced the senior Wentworth from the estates which he had high expectations of inheriting. It could be argued that the new Lord Raby had every right to be incensed, and he decided he had to make a stand. When a suitably large adjacent estate, which surrounded Stainborough Hall, was put up for sale in 1708, he bought it. The programme of improvements which took place was instigated by Lord Raby to 'cock a snook' at the owner of Wentworth Woodhouse and his family.

Stainborough Hall, which takes its name from an ancient earthwork the 'stone burgh', was built for Sir Gervase Cutler on the site of an older mansion, purchased by his great-grandfather Thomas Cutler in 1610 from the Everingham family, who had lived at Stainborough for over 350 years. Thomas's son Sir Gervase Cutler supported the Royalist cause during the Civil War, to his financial detriment, and died in the siege of Pontefract Castle. His son, the second Sir Gervase Cutler, was responsible for the rebuilding of Stainborough Hall, and although he increased the family's fortune the estate was heavily mortgaged. After Sir Gervase's death in 1703 financial pressures necessitated the sale of the entire Stainborough estate by his son, Henry Cutler. In 1708 Lord Raby paid Cutler £14,150, and became the estate's new owner.

Raby had risen rapidly, first in the army and then in the diplomatic service in the reigns of William III and Queen Anne. He amassed a considerable fortune and was ambassador in Berlin at the time he purchased Stainborough Hall. No sooner had he purchased the estate than he made preparations to build a superior house to Wentworth

Woodhouse. Berlin's chief architect, Johannes von Bodt (or Jean de Bodt, as he was known in his native France), a Huguenot refugee, agreed to design a new east-facing range in the new Baroque style to add to the existing Stainborough Hall. The architect never visited England to see his design executed, and Wentworth Castle is the only example of this famous continental architect's work in this country. The building programme took a considerable time to complete, and Lord Raby was away for much of the time: he owned other homes in London, Twickenham, Boughton in Northamptonshire and Freston in Suffolk. Construction work began at Stainborough, under the watchful eye of his brother, Peter Wentworth. Lord Raby succeeded in having the family's senior title revived in 1711, becoming the first Earl of Strafford of the second creation. During his lifetime he was described as a persistent supplicant for the Queen's favours, a complainer, an extremely boring speaker in the House of Lords and a downright snob. Jonathan Swift called him 'infinitely proud, and wholly illiterate'. The new Lord Strafford's fortune increased when he married a wealthy heiress in 1712. By 1714 the exterior work had been completed but work continued on the interior into the 1720s. Lord Strafford was able to spend more time overseeing the work and enjoying the comforts that his new home brought him, because on the death of Queen Anne in 1714 his public career came to an end, when the Whigs replaced the Tories in government and the Earl of Strafford, like many of his political allies, lost his influence at court.

The whole of the first floor of the new south range of Stainborough Hall was taken up by the 180 ft Long Gallery, designed by James Gibbs. William Thornton of York undertook most of the fitting out of the ground-floor rooms, and artists and craftsmen including John Goodyear and the French painter Clermont carried out work there. Strafford was very keen to ensure that the honours he had received were included in the design of the fabric of the building and every conceivable item was adorned with them. A visitor to Stainborough in 1717 nicknamed it the Stars and Garters, observing that 'There was not a suit of hangings, looking-glass nor cabinet, that was not adorned with those emblems of honour'. Whilst building work continued, the Earl turned his attention to the gardens and park, which he stocked with 300 deer. In 1728 he erected a sham fortification at Stainborough Low on the site of the ancient earthwork from which Stainborough took its name, and named this mock fortification Stainborough Castle. Many of the features he planned have long since disappeared but several remain, including Queen Anne's Obelisk, erected in her memory twenty years after her death.

The rivalry between the two branches of the Wentworth family continued and Lord Strafford decided he needed a grander name for his seat at Stainborough to highlight the importance of his station, and by 1731 Stainborough Hall had been provocatively renamed Wentworth Castle – and was then a vastly superior country seat to Wentworth Woodhouse. Having two 'castles' on the same estate and in close proximity to each other has added to the confusion of names. Today many people refer to Wentworth Castle as Stainborough Castle, without realising that Stainborough Castle lies on the hillside behind Wentworth Castle.

In 1723 Thomas Watson Wentworth junior succeeded his father to the Wentworth estates and began to build the West Front of Wentworth Woodhouse in the Baroque style to match the home of his kinsman at Stainborough. During the building programme which followed Thomas Watson Wentworth was created Knight of the Bath in 1725 and was elevated to the peerage by being created Baron Malton in 1728 and Earl of Malton in 1733, thereby equalling the Earl of Strafford in rank. Their attempts to outdo each other continued to be reflected in the buildings they had erected. Not only were their mansions enlarged and improved, but the most fantastic group of follies were constructed, and such buildings continued to be erected by their descendants. Although a very rich man, the Earl of Strafford's fortune and income was considerably less than the Earl of Malton's. Once rebuilding Wentworth Woodhouse had begun in earnest, the Wentworth ancestral home easily eclipsed the more modest, although extremely fine seat of the Earl of Strafford at Stainborough. The buildings and follies on the estate surrounding Wentworth Woodhouse have fared better than those at Stainborough, many of which have fallen into ruin or have been demolished.

Even before work had been completed on the West Front of Wentworth Woodhouse, the style in which it had been built was considered out of date, so an even more ambitious building programme was planned which resulted in the building of the colossal East Front. Lord Strafford must have been piqued when he saw this enormous project coming to fruition. He died in 1739, before work had been completed and before his great rival was given the superior title of Marquess of Rockingham in 1746.

The second Earl of Strafford, also called William Wentworth, did not go into politics and spent much of his time at Wentworth Castle. He was as enthusiastic a builder as his father. He had an obelisk erected in honour of Lady Mary Wortley-Montagu, who had introduced smallpox inoculation to this country from Turkey; this was positioned close to the mock castle. He decided to enlarge his home in an attempt to keep up with the Marquess of Rockingham at Wentworth Woodhouse, at least in style if not in scale, and had a thirteen-bay Palladian range constructed, facing south. It is generally believed that the Earl designed it himself, possibly with the assistance of a local architect. The work was overseen by Charles Ross, who had carried out work on the Earl's London home in St James's Square in 1748–9. Work commenced in 1759. John Platt II, the Rotherham mason and architect, carved the griffin crest and decoration on the pediment in 1762, and the capitals for the six giant Corinthian columns, for which he received £642 2s 2d. He had first worked at Wentworth Castle in 1755, when Lord Strafford asked him to examine the 'castle in the wilderness'. Stainborough Castle was in such a state of disrepair only twenty-seven years after it was built that Platt submitted an estimate of £96 8s 0d to restore the fabric. However, Lord Strafford thought the estimate too high, so Platt sent an amended estimate for 80 guineas, whilst informing his lordship that 'it will be a Troublesome affair & well deserves the whole Sum'. The exterior of the Palladian range was completed by 1764, although work on its interior continued. Platt was also responsible for carving several marble chimney pieces, and he continued to carry out work at Wentworth Castle until August 1765. A year later he was invited to a dinner by Lord Strafford, which was attended by the Duke of Cumberland amongst other notable people, to celebrate the completion of the Palladian range. Platt subsequently carried out work on the columns of the Corinthian Temple, overlooking the south lawn, and may well have worked on several other garden ornaments. Lord Strafford also had the formal gardens, which his father had had laid out by George London, the Royal gardener, altered and transformed into rolling parkland, as was the fashion in the second half of the 18th century. This gave his lordship further scope to construct follies and monuments at various strategic points throughout the estate. In 1789 Horace Walpole wrote that Wentworth Castle was 'my favourite of all great seats: such a variety of ground, of wood and water; and almost all executed and disposed with so much taste by the present earl'.

The second Earl of Strafford died without issue in 1791. The title was inherited by his cousin's son Frederick, who also had no children and died in 1799. The title Earl of Strafford once again became extinct. (The title was created for the third time for John

Byng in 1847, the great-grandson of the first Earl of the second creation.) On the death of the third Earl of Strafford the estate passed to his sister, Augusta Wentworth. On her death in 1802 it passed to Frederick Thomas William Vernon, the grandson of the second Earl. On inheriting the estate he assumed the surname of Vernon-Wentworth. He continued to build on the estate and was responsible for building the conservatory and improving the kitchen gardens. He died in 1885. His son Thomas built a wing on the north-west side of the original Stainborough Hall, to provide a new kitchen, servants' hall and additional bedroom and bathroom accommodation. He also installed electric light throughout Wentworth Castle. Thomas's son, Captain Bruce Vernon-Wentworth succeeded to the estate in 1902, and was responsible for many of the features in the present garden. He was a bachelor and in 1948 sold Wentworth Castle (but not the contents, some of which were auctioned), its outbuildings and 60 acres of the estate to Barnsley Education Committee for £26,000. He died in 1951. Wentworth Castle has remained in educational use ever since. Wentworth Castle is listed Grade I, being of architectural and historical importance. Its gardens are the only gardens in South Yorkshire to be so listed. The park, farmland and woods remain in the ownership and control of the Wentworth Estate.

Rockley, 1920s. The various historic country estates which have land in the vicinity of Rockley have largely become known towards the end of the 20th century as Worsborough Country Park, which is really concentrated around Worsborough Mill and Worsborough Reservoir. The entire area including Wentworth Castle and the Wentworth Estate offers some of the most beautiful countryside in the West Riding. (*Walker's Newsagents collection*)

The original Stainborough Hall, former home of the Cutler family, which still survives as part of Wentworth Castle, early 1970s. Lord Raby began building his grand east-facing range, the back of which can be seen to the left, attached to the hall, soon after he purchased the hall and estate from Henry Cutler in 1708. *(Author's collection)*

The magnificent Baroque south range of Wentworth Castle, designed by Jean de Bodt, seen here while it was a teacher training college. The balustrade in front of the mansion was one of the additions made by Captain Vernon-Wentworth, the last private owner of Wentworth Castle. *(Author's collection)*

A late 19th-century view of the south range of Wentworth Castle. This Palladian range is believed to have been designed by the second Earl of Strafford. *(Bob Dale collection)*

A view of the mock fortification known as Stainborough Castle, built on the Wentworth Castle estate by the first Earl of Strafford, on the hill which gave Stainborough its name. Shown during the early 20th century, the folly has now become more of a ruin. Two of the towers have fallen down and a third has its roof missing. It is a pity, but being in that condition fits in with the Medieval Romantic theme, which was the spirit in which it was originally built. The idea in Lord Strafford's mind was to create the illusion that his branch of the Wentworth family had been living on the estate for centuries. *(Bob Dale collection)*

Rockley Dam and surrounding area, 1920s. *(Walker's Newsagents collection)*

Friar Tail Wood, 1920s. To the right in the trees can be seen Rockley Woodhouse, and the 18th-century pavilion. *(Walker's Newsagents collection)*

The second Earl of Strafford decided to build what would be the last of the large structures outside the park. Rockley Woodhouse was built in 1747 in an embayment of Friar Tail Wood, south of the Serpentine beyond Rockley Dam. Constructed in a vaguely Adamesque style it consisted of a curved arcade, with a bay-fronted room at each end and a tower in the centre, surmounted by a cupola, bearing a weather vane. Originally used as a retreat for shooting parties, or as a place to rest awhile on a ramble through the estate, it ended its days being used largely by fishing parties. During open-cast mining in the 1950s Rockley Woodhouse was demolished, when a substantial part of Friar Tail Wood was destroyed – as was most of Green Spring Wood. This 1920s view was published as a postcard by Lichie Walker. (*Walker's Newsagents collection*)

A view of Cortonwood Colliery sidings, 25 January 1965. The mine which was at the centre of the 1984 strike can be seen here during a period of high productivity. Ted Ellis, guard, inspects the wagons prior to departure. The engine driver is A.V. Smith and the fireman P. Oliver. *(Edward Ellis collection)*

There are many smaller communities which are in some way connected with the development of the area which I have only been able to touch on. Hoyland Nether was until 1974 surrounded by several councils which administered the affairs of residents who had close connections with Hoyland – Wortley Rural District Council, Worsborough UDC and Wombwell UDC to name but three. *Around Hoyland* takes in some of the areas which were previously administered by these councils. This is a view of Burying Lane in winter during the early 1920s, taken from Alderthwaite. The postcard is erroneously titled Berrying Lane. *(Walker's Newsagents collection)*

Blacker Farm, Blacker Hill, *c. 1900. (Chris Thawley collection)*

Wentworth Road, Blacker Hill, *c. 1900. (Chris Thawley collection)*

Dovecliffe station, early 1900s. An isolated station with very attractive buildings, it closed in 1953. (*Chris Thawley collection*)

The Royal Albert Hall, Blacker Hill, *c.* 1920. Blacker Hill once had three public houses, but the Royal Albert is the only one that remains. (*Chris Thawley collection*)

The snug at the Royal Albert, Blacker Hill, *c. 1945. (Chris Thawley collection)*

The Gate House at Tingle Bridge, 1960s. The single-trace railway ran from Cortonwood Colliery to Elsecar Main. The Half Mile Road is directly to the right of the house. The Gate House was last occupied by Ted and Joyce Ellis. It became structurally unsafe and stood empty for several years before being demolished in the early 1970s. The Ellises bought Station House, the former station master's house at Wentworth station. *(Edward Ellis collection)*

The railway lift bridge and Knoll Beck Aqueduct, near Cortonwood Colliery, 1949. *(Edward Ellis collection)*

Cortonwood signal box. Signalwoman Joyce Ellis stands outside the box and Signalwoman Rich is in the doorway. *(Edward Ellis collection)*

Jump and district war memorial, 1920s. *(Walker's Newsagents collection)*

The signal box at Skiers Spring, 1960s. This two-shift box was operated by Signalmen J. Stancey and C. Womersley. *(Edward Ellis collection)*

The turnpike, approaching the Hoyland and Elsecar turn off near Wentworth station, 1970. The sign on the railway bridge was a familiar sight for many years. *(Joan Masheder collection)*

The staff of Birdwell and Hoyland Common station, 1950s. *(Chris Thawley collection)*

The Wath-upon-Dearne to Elsecar train at Tingle Bridge, driven by H. Booth of Mexborough, 1950s. *(Edward Ellis collection)*

A group of workmen at Skiers Spring Brickworks, *c.* 1880. The brickworks opened in 1887 and closed in 1919. *(Jack Howse collection)*

Junction 36 of the M1 motorway looking north, 1971. Birdwell can be seen to the right of the motorway, which winds its way through the Wentworth estate from Birdwell towards Barnsley and beyond. The obelisk at Birdwell, erected in 1775 by the second Earl of Strafford, can be seen in the right background. (*Joan Masheder collection*)

A composite postcard view of sights around Hoyland, published in the 1920s by Lichie Walker. (*Walker's Newsagents collection*)

ACKNOWLEDGEMENTS

My Personal Assistant Mr John D. Murray, Mr Paul T. Langley Welch, Mr David Walker and Mrs Christine Walker of Walker's Newsagents, Hoyland, Mr Clifford and Mrs Margaret Willoughby, Mr Herbert and Mrs Doreen Howse, Mrs Joan Hopson, Mr Peter Marsh for his assistance in providing detailed information concerning Tankersley Park and other useful information, Mrs Joan Masheder, Mr Ivan P. Walker, Mrs Margaret Gaddass, Mr George Hardy, Mrs Val Noble, Mr Bob Mortimer, Mr Edward Ellis, Mrs Joyce Ellis, Mr Jack (John) Howse, Mrs Martha Nelder, the late Mr Frank Kelly, Mr Eric Hill, Mr Chris Thawley, of the Royal Albert Hotel, Blacker Hill, Mrs Brenda Gill, the late the Hon. Lady Hastings, Mr Guy Canby FRICS, Agent to the Fitzwilliam Wentworth Estates, Mrs Anne Howse, Mr Keith Froggatt, Mrs Julie Wiggett, Miss Tracy P. Deller, Master Ricki S. Deller, Miss Joanna C. Murray Deller, the Earl of Longford, Mr Ralph Walker, Mr Bob (R.A.) Dale and Mrs Kath (Kathleen) Dale, the late Councillor Dennis Eaden, Geoffrey Hazelwood JP, Mrs Christine Short, Tony Briggs of Harvey and Richardson, Hoyland, Sheila Margaret Ottley, Michael F. Bedford, Arthur K. Clayton BEM, Clarence Walker, Harry Grounds of Class Method Ltd, Paul McBride, Paul McDonald, Mr Vince Linnane, Mr Jeremy Hale, Mr Sean Lambe, Simon Fletcher, Annabel Fearnley, Olwen Greany and Anne Bennett.

Paul T. Langley Welch, who has taken the 1999 photographs included in this book, works as a freelance commercial and theatrical photographer. Since 1983 he has been working for such companies as the National Theatre, the Old Vic and the Royal Shakespeare Company. Commercial clients include United Distillers, the National Tourist Board, the Arts Council of Great Britain, British Telecom and F1 Racing (Silverstone). He has also produced films in conjunction with Pauline Turner for PPM Productions, for the National Tourist Board.